LEAVING CERTIFICATE POETRY ANTHOLOGY FOR ORDINARY LEVEL 2007

NEW
DISCOVERY

PATRICK MURRAY
KEVIN MCDERMOTT
MARY SLATTERY

EDCO
THE EDUCATIONAL COMPANY

First published 2005

The Educational Company
Ballymount Road
Walkinstown
Dublin 12

A trading unit of Smurfit Ireland Limited

Approved Quality
System

The
paper used in
this book comes
from Managed
Forests in
Northern
Europe
For
every
tree
felled, at
least one new
tree is planted

Design and layout: Identikit
Cover photograph: Getty Images
Printed in Ireland by Profile Lithoprint Ltd.

0 1 2 3 4 5 6 7 8 9

FOREWORD

This anthology, which includes all the poems prescribed for the Ordinary Level English Leaving Certificate Examinations of 2007, has been prepared by three experienced teachers of English. Each of the contributors has been able to concentrate on a limited number of the prescribed poets and their work, thus facilitating a high standard of research and presentation.

Guidelines are given which set each poem in context. In addition, each poem is accompanied by a glossary and appropriate explorations, designed to allow the student to find his/her authentic response to the material. Relevant biographical details are provided for each poet.

Guidelines are included for students on approaching the Unseen Poetry section of the course. There is also advice on approaching the prescribed question in the examination. Students will also find the glossary of poetic terms a valuable resource in reading and responding to poetry.

The poetry course for Leaving Certificate English demands a personal and active engagement from the student reader. We hope that this anthology makes that engagement possible and encourages students to explore the wider world of poetry for themselves.

CONTENTS

W. B. YEATS

ACKNOWLEDGEMENTS

The publishers wish to thank the following for kind permission to reproduce the poems in this book:

'For Heidi with Blue Hair' by Fleur Adcock from *Poems 1960–2000* published by Bloodaxe Books, 2000

'It Ain't What You Do It's What It Does To You' from *Zoom* (1989) by Simon Armitage, reproduced by kind permission of Bloodaxe Books.

'Funeral Blues' by W. H. Auden by kind permission of Faber and Faber.

'The Voice' from *Friend of Heraclitus* by Patricia Beer published by Carcanet Press Limited.

'The Fish', 'The Filling Station' from *The Complete Poems: 1927–1979* by Elizabeth Bishop. Copyright © 1979, 1983 by Alice Helen Methfessel. Reprinted by kind permission of Farrar, Straus and Giroux, LLC.

'Jasmine' from *Digging Towards the Light'* by Paddy Bushe, reproduced by kind permission of the author and the publishers Daedalus Press.

'Valentine' from *Mean Time* by Carol Ann Duffy published by Anvil Press Poetry in 1993 by kind permission of Anvil Press Poetry.

'Going Home to Mayo' by Paul Durcan reproduced by kind permission of the Poet.

'Aunt Helen', 'Preludes' from *Collected Poems 1909–1962* by T. S. Eliot by kind permission of the publishers Faber and Faber and the Eliot Estate.

'Acquainted with the Night', 'The Road Not Taken', 'Out, out', from *The Poetry of Robert Frost* edited by Edward Connery Lathem © 1928, 1969, by Henry Holt and Company © 1936, 1942, 1956 by Robert Frost © 1964, 1970 by Lesley Frost Ballantine. Reprinted by kind permission of Henry Holt and Co. LLC.

'Shancoduff', From *The Great Hunger*, 'A Christmas Childhood', 'On Raglan Road' by Patrick Kavanagh reprinted with the permission of the Trustees of the Estate of the late Katherine B. Kavanagh, through the Jonathan Williams Literary Agency.

'What Were They Like?' from *Selected Poems* by Denise Levertov, reproduced by kind permission of Pollinger Limited and the proprietor, New Directions.

'The Locket', 'The Cage', 'Like dolmens around my childhood', from *Collected Poems* (1995) by John Montague reproduced by kind permission of the author and The Gallery Press, Loughcrew, Oldcastle, Co. Meath, Ireland.

'Strawberries' from *Collected Poems* by Edwin Morgan, published by Carcanet Press Limited.

'Anseo' by Paul Muldoon from *New Selected Poems 1968–94* by kind permission of the publishers Faber and Faber and the author.

'The Reading Lesson' from *Collected Poems* (2000) by Richard Murphy by kind permission of the author and The Gallery Press, Loughcrew, Oldcastle, Co. Meath, Ireland.

'Wolves in the Zoo' by Howard Nemerov reproduced by kind permission of Mrs Margaret Nemerov.

'The Present Moment' from *The Father* by Sharon Olds, copyright 1992 by Sharon Olds. Reproduced by kind permission of Alfred A. Knopf, a division of Random House Inc.

'Child', 'The Arrival of the Bee Box', from *Collected Poems* by Syliva Plath, published by Faber and Faber. Reproduced by kind permission of the publishers.

'Adlestrop' from *Collected Poems* by Edward Thomas, Oxford University Press, edited by Professor R. George Thomas.

'The Lake Isle of Innisfree', 'The Wild Swans at Coole', 'An Irish Airman Foresees his Death', by W. B. Yeats by kind permission of A. P. Watts on behalf of Michael B. Yeats.

The photos of the poets are reproduced with kind permission of Getty Images and Corbis.

Despite their very best persistent efforts, in the case of some copyright pieces, the publishers have not been able to contact the copyright holders, but the publishers will be glad to make the appropriate arrangements with them as soon as they make contact.

FLEUR ADCOCK

B. 1934

BIOGRAPHY

Fleur Adcock was born near Auckland in New Zealand in 1934. Much of her childhood was spent in wartime England where she was educated. After the war, she and her family returned to New Zealand. She completed her studies at Victoria University in Wellington. Later she returned to England and worked as a librarian and arts administrator.

Fleur Adcock has published several collections of poetry, amongst them *The Incident Book* (1986), which contains 'For Heidi with Blue Hair'. *Selected Poems* was published in 1983 and she has also published *Poems 1960–2000*.

Adcock's work has been awarded many prizes, and she is one of the most popular women poets of recent years.

FOR HEIDI WITH BLUE HAIR

When you dyed your hair blue
(or, at least, ultramarine
for the clipped sides, with a crest
of jet-black spikes on top)
you were sent home from school   5

because, as the headmistress put it,
although dyed hair was not
specifically forbidden, yours
was, apart from anything else,
not done in the school colours.   10

Tears in the kitchen, telephone-calls
to school from your freedom-loving father:
'She's not a punk in her behaviour;
it's just a style.' (You wiped your eyes,
also not in a school colour.)   15

'She discussed it with me first—
we checked the rules.' 'And anyway, Dad,
it cost twenty-five dollars.
Tell them it won't wash out—
not even if I wanted to try.'   20

It would have been unfair to mention
your mother's death, but that
shimmered behind the arguments.
The school had nothing else against you;
the teachers twittered and gave in.   25

Next day your black friend had hers done
in grey, white and flaxen yellow—
the school colours precisely:
an act of solidarity, a witty
tease. The battle was already won.   30

GLOSSARY

2 *ultramarine*: a deep blue

13 *punk*: a follower of punk-rock, a style of music popular in the 1970s which had rather aggressive lyrics. Punks were thought to be violent people

27 *flaxen*: pale yellow

29 *solidarity*: joining together, support

GUIDELINES

The poet herself tells us that 'For Heidi with Blue Hair' was written in response to a real incident experienced by her god-daughter, Heidi, who had moved with her father (after the death of her mother) to live in Australia.

The poem speaks directly to Heidi. Her hairstyle is described in the first stanza. It seems to be a typical 1970s 'punk' style, short on the sides and spiked on top, dyed dark blue and black. Next the poem tells of the reaction of the headmistress. She objects to Heidi's hair for the rather absurd reason that it is not dyed in the school colours. We can hear the voice of the headmistress behind the seemingly casual phrase 'apart from anything else'. What else? Perhaps this suggests that she is not being completely open about the reasons why she objects to the hairstyle.

The third stanza continues the story from the point of view of Heidi and her father. We see that they do not share in the headmistress's opinion. By using direct conversation the poet makes the situation more real to the reader, like dialogue in a play. The relationship between Heidi and her father seems to be a supportive one. There is no suggestion that he wants her to break the school rules, though he is described as 'freedom-loving'.

By referring to the death of Heidi's mother in the fifth stanza, the poet shifts our sympathy completely to Heidi and away from the school. It has the effect of making us look at Heidi's small act of rebellion in a new way. We now see it as a means of reacting to the stress of bereavement. In this stanza the poet makes her own feelings clear. The attitude of the school is seen as rather negative, as suggested also by the word 'twittered', an unflattering description of the teachers concerned.

The final stanza makes an amusing comment on the whole affair. Heidi's friend's hairstyle is intended as an act of support for Heidi but it is also a challenge to the authority of the school. They will now have to find another reason for disapproving of the hairstyle, since it is now done in 'the school colours'.

The poem ends with the 'battle' metaphor. It suggests that Heidi and her friends have been the winners here. Individuality has won out over conformity.

QUESTIONS

1 What impression of the headmistress and the school does the poem give?
2 What sort of people are Heidi and her father? Support your answer by reference to the poem.
3 In your view, why does the poet say, 'You wiped your eyes, / also not in a school colour'?
4 What does the speaker of the poem think of the school rule, in your view? How do we know?
5 How would you describe the poet's use of language in this poem?
6 Do you think the poem gives a realistic picture of teenagers and their attitudes? Explain your answer.
7 Do you like this poem? Give reasons for your opinion.

SIMON ARMITAGE

B. 1963

BIOGRAPHY

Simon Armitage was born in 1963 in Huddersfield and grew up in West Yorkshire. He studied geography at Portsmouth Polytechnic and later social work and psychology at Manchester University. He has worked as a shelf stacker, disc jockey and lathe operator. For some time he worked as a probation officer. He is now a freelance writer.

He has presented poetry programmes for the BBC, worked as an editor and taught at the University of Leeds and the University of Iowa, USA. In 2000 he was writer-in-residence at the Millennium Dome in London.

Armitage is the author of nine volumes of poetry, including *Zoom!* (1989), *Kid* (1992) and *Cloudcuckooland* (1996). He has also written four stage plays and two novels. He has received many awards for his writing, including the Forward Poetry Prize in 1992. In 1994 he was named *Sunday Times* Writer of the Year.

IT AIN'T WHAT YOU DO
IT'S WHAT IT DOES TO YOU

I have not bummed across America
with only a dollar to spare, one pair
of busted Levi's and a bowie knife.
I have lived with thieves in Manchester.

I have not padded through the Taj Mahal,   5
barefoot, listening to the space between
each footfall picking up and putting down
its print against the marble floor. But I

skimmed flat stones across Black Moss on a day
so still I could hear each set of ripples   10
as they crossed. I felt each stones' inertia
spend itself against the water; then sink.

I have not toyed with a parachute chord
while perched on the lip of a light aircraft;
but I held the wobbly head of a boy   15
at the day centre, and stroked his fat hands.

And I guess that the tightness in the throat
and the tiny cascading sensation
somewhere inside us are both part of that
sense of something else. That feeling, I mean.   20

GLOSSARY

3 *Levi's*: a brand of jeans

3 *bowie knife*: a strong, one-edged dagger knife

5 *Taj Mahal*: the most famous building in India, the magnificent mausoleum at Agra

9 *Black Moss*: a river on the border between Yorkshire and Lancashire.

11 *inertia*: stillness

18 *cascading*: falling (like a waterfall)

GUIDELINES

'It Ain't What You Do It's What It Does To You' is from the collection *Zoom!* (1989). The title of the poem echoes the song 'It ain't what you do it's the way that you do it'. Simon Armitage's work as a probation officer helps to explain some of his references in the poem.

The poem tells us about some of the adventurous things other people have done that the poet has not. For example, he hasn't travelled across America with little or no money, visited the Taj Mahal in India (one of the seven wonders of the world) or made a parachute jump from an aeroplane. Even though he has not been to India, he describes it in some detail, as if someone had told him about it. You can sense a certain regret, perhaps, that he has missed out on this particular experience, from the language he uses to convey its quietness and spirituality.

But he has his own experiences to relate. The things he has done may seem ordinary, such as living among thieves (we remember that he was a probation officer for a time), or skimming stones across a river. As in the description of the Taj Mahal, he makes use of the sounds of words to help us share in the experience of skimming stones. Notice the amount of 's' sounds he uses that create a musical effect, echoing the sound of water. It is as if this simple action was as significant to him as a visit to India would have been.

In the fourth stanza he mentions perhaps the most thrilling or dangerous thing he has not done – the parachute jump. But what he *has* done is communicate with, and comfort, another human being. The words suggest that this boy is special, perhaps unable to communicate by speech. It is a moving image that contrasts with the danger and excitement of the first two lines of the stanza.

In the last stanza the poet tries to express the effect that his own, more ordinary experiences have had on him. He uses his senses to get across the idea that these experiences have caused him to feel as emotional as more exciting adventures might have done. He suggests, too, that these feelings may also have a deeper, more spiritual significance, what he calls 'that / sense of something else'. The words are vague, as if he is attempting to describe the indescribable, and realises how difficult it is.

THE THEME OF THE POEM

The title of the poem gives us a good idea as to what its theme may be. What we actually do may not matter very much. What matters is how we respond to it and what effect it has on us as human beings. That is how we achieve fulfillment.

QUESTIONS

1 Why do you think the poet chooses the particular experiences that he has missed? What do they have in common with each other?

2 Do you think he regrets not having these experiences? Explain your answer.

3 Why did skimming the stones across the river and holding the boy's head at the day centre mean so much to him? What might these experiences have in common with each other, if anything?

4 What kind of feeling do you think Armitage is describing in the last stanza? Does he describe it well, in your opinion?

5 Which of the experiences described in the poem would you yourself like to share? Explain your answer.

6 From your reading of the poem, what sort of person do you imagine the speaker to be?

7 Does this poem make you think about life in a new way?

8 Do you think this poem appeals to young people in particular? Give reasons for your view.

W. H. AUDEN

1907−73

BIOGRAPHY

Wystan Hugh Auden was born in York, England, in February 1907. He was educated at St Edmund's School, Surrey, and at Christ Church College, Oxford. As a young man he worked as a schoolmaster in England. He also spent time in Berlin in the 1930s. He took part in the Spanish Civil war in 1937 as a stretcher-bearer, fighting on the Republican side. In 1939 he emigrated to America and became an American citizen in 1946.

Auden lectured at several colleges in America and England. He was Professor of Poetry at Oxford University from 1956 to 1960.

Auden published many collections of poetry and received numerous awards for his work, including the Pulitzer Prize in Poetry in 1948. His intellectual gifts and his ability to write in many different forms was extraordinary. His output ranges from light verse, ballads and songs to serious poems, political commentary, and even opera libretti. In his work as a critic he edited a huge anthology, *Poets of the English Language,* published in New York in 1950. By the time of his death in 1973 he was regarded as one of the leading poets of the twentieth century.

As a homosexual, Auden was forced, due to the conventions of the times, to conceal the sex of his beloved in his love poems. His love poems, like 'Funeral Blues', have a wonderful delicacy and tenderness.

FUNERAL BLUES

Stop all the clocks, cut off the telephone,
Prevent the dog from barking with a juicy bone,
Silence the pianos and with muffled drum
Bring out the coffin, let the mourners come.

Let aeroplanes circle moaning overhead   5
Scribbling on the sky the message He Is Dead,
Put the crêpe bows round the white necks of the public doves,
Let the traffic policemen wear black cotton gloves.

He was my North, my South, my East and West,
My working week and my Sunday rest,   10
My noon, my midnight, my talk, my song;
I thought that love would last for ever: I was wrong.

The stars are not wanted now: put out every one;
Pack up the moon and dismantle the sun;
Pour away the ocean and sweep up the wood.   15
For nothing now can ever come to any good.

GLOSSARY

title *Blues*: a slow, sad song

7 *Put the…doves*: flocks of doves were once let loose to mark public occasions of celebration or mourning. Crepe is a thin, silky material, dyed black in times of mourning (also called crape)

14 *dismantle*: take to pieces

GUIDELINES

This poem is the ninth song of 'Twelve Songs' which Auden wrote in 1936. The first two stanzas were used initially in a play written by Auden and his friend, Christopher Isherwood, *The Ascent of F6*. In the play the context was political; the lines satirised the love of a people for a dead leader. Auden later decided to use them as the start of this more personal love song.

The speaker expresses deep grief at the death of his loved one. He wishes that the world could come to an end. All the sounds of everyday life should be silenced, except the sound of the drum as the coffin is brought out.

The sense of grief becomes ever more overwhelming as the poem progresses. The speaker wants public recognition of the death of his beloved, as if it was a tremendous loss to the whole world.

The third stanza is more personal in tone. The speaker uses moving metaphors to convey what his beloved meant to him. The effect of these lines is to pay a remarkable tribute to the loved one. The last line of this stanza is simply expressed (all of the words are of one syllable only) but they leave an impression of utter desolation.

The speaker can see no future, no value in the world since his beloved is not there. Elemental images such as the stars, sun and ocean suggest the depth of his grief. These very elements are of no use to him now. He would like to see them destroyed. The grief-stricken tone of the final line seems to sum up what he feels.

THE SOUND PATTERNS OF THE POEM

The sound patterns contribute to its musical effect as a 'song'. The poet makes use of end-rhyme, assonance (rhyme of internal vowel sounds), alliteration and long vowel sounds (e.g. 'moaning') that echo the sound of mourning. The simple language and personal expression add to the atmosphere of love and loss.

QUESTIONS

1 How does the speaker of the poem express his grief at the death of his beloved?

2 Which lines best convey his feelings, in your view? Give a reason for your choice.

3 Do you think the poem works well as a love poem and as a poem written after someone's death (i.e. as an elegy)?

4 Explore the sound patterns of the poem. Would you agree that it is a musical poem, as the title suggests?

5 How did you respond to this poem?

6 You have been asked to suggest a poem to be included in an anthology of love poems. You recommend this one. Explain why.

PATRICIA BEER

1919–1999

BIOGRAPHY

Patricia Beer was born in Devon in 1919, into a Plymouth Brethren family. (Plymouth Brethren is the name of a religious sect founded in 1827. It has a strict moral code and emphasises the dangers of sin.) She grew up in Devon and settled there for the last decades of her life.

She taught English literature in Italy and in Goldsmith's College, London.

Her first book of poetry, *The Loss of Magyar*, was published when she was 40. Throughout the 1960s and early 1970s she published three additional poetry collections. In 1968, she resigned from her teaching job to become a full-time writer. Her autobiographical book, *Mrs Beer's House*, evokes her childhood in Devon. She also published a critical study of women writers. Her 1978 novel *Moon's Ottery* described life in a Devon village at the time of the Spanish Armada. When her collection *Friend of Heraclitus* won an award on its publication in 1973, she said that the recognition gave her 'an agreeable sense of persistence'.

Given that her career as a poet extended over forty years, much of Patricia Beer's poetry has the traditional element of rhyme, but she also wrote syllabic verse and free verse. Patricia Beer was writing up to the time of her death. Her last book of poetry, *Autumn*, was published in 1997.

THE VOICE

When God took my aunt's baby boy, a merciful neighbour
Gave her a parrot. She could not have afforded one
But now bought a new cage as brilliant as the bird,
And turned her back on the idea of other babies.

He looked unlikely. In her house his scarlet feathers   5
Stuck out like a jungle, though his blue ones blended
With the local pottery which carried messages
Like 'Du ee help yerself to crame, me handsome.'

He said nothing when he arrived, not a quotation
From pet-shop gossip or a sailor's oath, no sound   10
From someone's home: the telephone or car-door slamming,
And none from his: tom-tom, war-cry or wild beast roaring.

He came from silence but was ready to become noise.
My aunt taught him nursery rhymes morning after morning.
He learnt Miss Muffett, Jack and Jill, Little Jack Horner,   15
Including her jokes; she used to say turds and whey.

A genuine Devon accent is not easy. Actors
Cannot do it. He could though. In his court clothes
He sounded like a farmer, as her son might have.
He sounded like our family. He fitted in.   20

Years went by. We came and went. A day or two
Before he died, he got confused, and muddled up
His rhymes. Jack Horner ate his pail of water.
The spider said what a good boy he was. I wept.

He had never seemed puzzled by the bizarre events   25
He spoke of. But the last day he turned his head towards us
With the bewilderment of death upon him. Said
'Broke his crown' and 'Christmas pie'. And tumbled after.

My aunt died the next winter, widowed, childless, pitied
And patronised. I cannot summon up her voice at all.   30
She would not have expected it to be remembered
After so long. But I can still hear his.

GLOSSARY

8 *'Du ee help yerself to crame, me handsome'*: 'Do help yourself to cream, my handsome.'
Tourism in Devon plays upon its past associations with pirates and smugglers

16 *turds and whey*: in the nursery rhyme, 'Little Miss Muffett', the opening lines are:
'Little Miss Muffett sat on a tuffet / Eating her curds and whey'. Curds are the
thickened or cheese part of milk. A turd is a lump of excrement or dung

30 *patronised*: treated kindly by those who considered themselves her superiors

GUIDELINES

'The Voice' tells the story of the poet's aunt and her parrot, in a direct, straight-forward way that combines humour and irony. The setting of the poem is Devon, a part of England associated with pirates and pirate ships.

The opening stanza tells the reader how the parrot came to the narrator's aunt. Some readers might find it amusing; others might find it almost cruel. Readers may also differ in their assessment of the style of the poem. Is the language too flat and ordinary, or does it capture the flow of everyday speech?

The opening statement of Stanza 2, 'He looked unlikely', shows Beer's talent for pithy, clever summations of a situation. The stanza suggests that the parrot both stands out and blends in, in the aunt's house.

The idea of belonging to two worlds is developed in Stanza 3. The parrot, we are told, did not speak when he came to the aunt's house. He said nothing of the things he might have heard in his adopted home, nor did he imitate the sounds of home. The opening of the fourth stanza is a well-balanced line, neatly contrasting silence and noise: 'He came from silence but was ready to become noise'.

Stanza 5 is one of the most interesting stanzas in the poem. It is developed from another contrast, this time between the 'court clothes' of the parrot and his Devon farmer's accent. The narrator says the parrot 'sounded like our family'. More tellingly the narrator says that the parrot sounded 'as her son might have'. This is the emotional centre of the poem.

The story gathers pace in the sixth stanza and we are brought to the day before the parrot died. The tone softens, as the narrator describes the parrot's confusion. The final 'I wept' of the stanza appears to be without irony. The account of the parrot's death continues into Stanza 7. Arguably lines 25–27 are the best lines in the poem, with their array of sounds and sound correspondences and the admirable phrase, 'the bewilderment of death'.

The final stanza deserves careful reading. Does the aunt live on in the remembered voice of the parrot? Or is the narrator's remembrance of the parrot a final insult to the pitied and patronised aunt? Is 'The Voice' an exercise in warm affection, or an exercise in cruel indifference? Or is it something in between?

QUESTIONS

1 The first stanza tells us the story of how the parrot came to the poet's aunt. Comment on the statement, 'When Good took my aunt's baby boy' and the use of 'merciful' to describe the neighbour.

2 What, do you think, caused the aunt to turn her back 'on the idea of other babies'?

3 'He looked unlikely.' What do you think is the tone implied in this phrase? Where else is this tone apparent?

4 In Stanza 5, what is the importance of the parrot's Devon accent? From reading this stanza, what part does the parrot play in the aunt's life?

5 At the end of Stanza 6, the poet says 'I wept'. What is the cause of this grief? Are you surprised by it?

6 a) 'My aunt died next winter.' Does the poet want us to connect the aunt's death with the death of the parrot?
   b) In the final stanza, the poet's aunt is 'pitied / And patronised'. Does the poet share these attitudes?

7 How do you read the final sentence of the poem? Is it humorous, ironic, insulting? Explain your answer.

8 Would you agree that the poem displays a sense of humour that is almost cruel? Explain your answer.

9 What phrases or lines do you like most? Explain your choice.

10 'In remembering the parrot, the poet remembers her aunt.' Discuss.

11 Do you think 'The Voice' sounds enough like a poem? Explain your answer.

ELIZABETH BISHOP

1911–1979

BIOGRAPHY

Elizabeth Bishop was born on 8 February, 1911, in Worcester, Massachusetts. She was the only child of William T. Bishop and Gertrude May Bulmer Bishop. William Bishop, who was vice-president of his father's successful building firm, died of Bright's disease when Elizabeth was only eight months old. Her mother, Gertrude, was so traumatised by her husband's death that it led to the mental breakdown which resulted in her being hospitalised five years later. Elizabeth never saw her mother again, although she lived until 1934.

Although Elizabeth Bishop left published accounts of only two memories of her life with her mother (one of them a short reference in her poem 'First Death in Nova Scotia'), it is clear that the experience left an indelible impression on her, influencing her emotional life and possibly accounting for her later struggles with depression and alcoholism.

Elizabeth was cared for initially by her maternal grandparents at Great Village, a tiny town in Nova Scotia, a time she recollected later with affection. Her grandparents were simple and loving people, and there was a family of aunts and uncles who were kind and caring. However, in 1917 her paternal grandparents, the wealthy Bishops, arrived in Great Village by train to take the six-year old Elizabeth back to live with them in Worcester. Her departure was so sudden that she recalled it as a 'kidnapping' from the happy home she knew to a much more austere environment, a change so violent that it seems to have created a sense of loss in the child that remained with her as an adult.

Her unhappiness showed itself in the many illnesses she suffered from, including asthma, bronchitis and eczema. The Bishops felt unable to cope with her after only nine months. Her mother's older sister, Aunt Maude, rescued the ill and nervous child by taking her to live with her and her husband in the upstairs apartment of a run-down tenement in an impoverished neighbourhood in Revere, Massachusetts. Later, Elizabeth said that Aunt Maude had saved her life.

Because of her illnesses, Elizabeth had very little formal schooling before the age of fourteen. Her formal education, paid for by the Bishops, began at Walnut Hill School for Girls. Academically she made great progress. Her literary gifts were apparent by this time and she wrote fiction and poetry for the school magazine. By the time she attended the exclusive all-girls' college at Vassar, in New York, where she majored in English literature, she was already considered to have great talent. She was also an accomplished musician and a talented painter.

On graduating from college Elizabeth lived in New York, writing poems for small magazines and using money from her inheritance to travel to France, England, North Africa, Spain and Italy. In 1938 she moved to Key West, Florida. In 1946 her first book of poems, *North & South,* the fruit of ten years' work, received the Houghton Mifflin Poetry Award. Awarded a Guggenheim Fellowship in 1947, she became Consultant in Poetry at the Library of Congress.

Her life changed again in 1951 when she met Lota de Macedo Soares on a visit to Brazil. The two women settled together near Rio de Janeiro in a lesbian relationship that was to last until Lota's death in 1967. Elizabeth Bishop always said that this was the happiest time of her life. For the first time she had a home and a sense of family with Lota's adopted children.

Her second book, *A Cold Spring,* was published in 1955. Combined with *North & South,* it won the Pulitzer Prize for Poetry. Her travels continued. In 1961 she took a trip down the Amazon to see Indian tribes. She also visited Mexico and was a frequent visitor to Europe. Her literary reputation was recognised by the Fellowship of the Academy of American Poets awarded in 1964, while in 1965 her third collection, *Questions of Travel,* appeared. After Lota's death she lived for a year in San Francisco, then taught for a number of years at Harvard University, Cambridge, Massachusetts. In 1976, following her pattern of producing a book of poems every ten years, she published *Geography III.* Numerous prizes and awards followed until her death in Boston in 1979. In 1991, her *Complete Poems* were published.

THE FISH

I caught a tremendous fish
and held him beside the boat
half out of water, with my hook
fast in a corner of his mouth.
He didn't fight.   5
He hadn't fought at all.
He hung a grunting weight,
battered and venerable
and homely. Here and there
his brown skin hung in strips   10
like ancient wallpaper,
and its pattern of darker brown
was like wallpaper:
shapes like full-blown roses
stained and lost through age.   15
He was speckled with barnacles,
fine rosettes of lime,
and infested
with tiny white sea-lice,
and underneath two or three   20
rags of green weed hung down.
While his gills were breathing in
the terrible oxygen
—the frightening gills,
fresh and crisp with blood,   25
that can cut so badly—
I thought of the coarse white flesh
packed in like feathers,
the big bones and the little bones,
the dramatic reds and blacks   30
of his shiny entrails,
and the pink swim-bladder
like a big peony.

I looked into his eyes
which were far larger than mine   35
but shallower, and yellowed,
the irises backed and packed
with tarnished tinfoil
seen through the lenses
of old scratched isinglass.   40
They shifted a little, but not
to return my stare.
—It was more like the tipping
of an object toward the light.
I admired his sullen face,   45
the mechanism of his jaw,
and then I saw
that from his lower lip
—if you could call it a lip—
grim, wet, and weaponlike,   50
hung five old pieces of fish-line,
or four and a wire leader
with the swivel still attached,
with all their five big hooks
grown firmly in his mouth.   55
A green line, frayed at the end
where he broke it, two heavier lines,
and a fine black thread
still crimped from the strain and snap
when it broke and he got away.   60
Like medals with their ribbons
frayed and wavering,
a five-haired beard of wisdom
trailing from his aching jaw.
I stared and stared   65
and victory filled up
the little rented boat,
from the pool of bilge
where oil had spread a rainbow
around the rusted engine   70

to the bailer rusted orange,
the sun-cracked thwarts,
the oarlocks on their strings,
the gunnels — until everything
was rainbow, rainbow, rainbow!   75
And I let the fish go.

GLOSSARY

16 *barnacles*: crustaceans or shellfish that cling to rocks, large fish etc

31 *entrails*: inner parts of the fish

33 *peony*: a large, showy flower

40 *isinglass*: a whitish, semi-transparent gelatinous substance

52 *wire leader*: short piece of wire connecting fishhook and fishline

53 *swivel*: a ring or link that turns round on a pin or neck

59 *crimped*: curled

68 *bilge*: filth that collects in the bottom of a boat

71 *bailer*: a bucket for ladling water out of a boat

72 *thwarts*: the seat or bench that the rowers sit on

73 *oarlocks*: a device for holding and balancing the oar on the side of a boat

74 *gunnels*: gunwale, the upper edge of a boat's side

GUIDELINES

'The Fish' was written when Bishop lived in Florida in the 1930s. It is included in her first collection, *North & South*. As with so many of her poems, it is based on a real experience that she had of catching a large Caribbean jewfish at Key West.

The poem describes in detail what the fish looked like, using some unusual and original images that appeal to our visual and tactile senses. The poet gives us a realistic picture of the fish, seeing him not only in imaginative terms but also taking care to present him as he really is, with his fishy texture and physical characteristics. Her description bears out the poet and critic Randall Jarrell's statement that her poems should have 'I have seen it' written about them.

Bishop is also concerned with her own response to capturing the fish. This goes beyond the conventional delight at having 'caught a tremendous fish'. As we read through the poem, we can trace her growing interest and emotional involvement in the fish and his struggle, past and present. Despite the barrier between human and animal, she begins to empathise with him. The language she uses suggests that she recognises the difficulties he has had, and his achievements in overcoming them.

From the beginning, the fish seems more than just a creature of nature. Bishop gives him some human characteristics, as in a traditional fable. In such fables, an encounter between animal and human contains a message or a moral. It may be that the lesson of the poem, the reason why she finally 'let the fish go', is connected with her awareness that the fish has a moral right to his own survival. Such an interpretation would suggest that Bishop had a recognition of the complex relationship human beings have with the natural world. In this context the idea of 'victory' and the image of the rainbow at the end of the poem have rich connotations. Randall Jarrell responded to the moral choice facing Bishop in the poem and what it revealed about its creator:

> She is morally so attractive in poems like 'The Fish' , because she understands so well that the wickedness and confusion of the age can explain and extenuate other people's wickedness and confusion, but not, for you, your own.

If we accept this reading of the poem, it would reveal Bishop's modern, ecologically aware attitude to nature, reflected also in poems such as 'The Armadillo'.

It has been suggested also that the poem dramatises how the creative imagination of a poet works by seeking to enter into an experience outside her own, recognising by careful observing the 'otherness' of the fish, and finally allowing the imagination to let go of whatever theme it has been dealing with.

These are interesting issues that you might consider further when you have read through the poem.

The poem is written as one long narrative with a clear beginning, progression and ending. It is unrhymed, as appropriate to create the impression of the speaking voice, with the exception of the last two lines. The rhyming couplet gives a sense of closure. The metre Bishop chooses is dimeter, with two stresses per line (as in 'He didn't fight') or trimeter with three stresses ('He hadn't fought at all'). This form of metre echoes speech rhythms and is particularly suitable for telling a story.

QUESTIONS

1 'I caught a tremendous fish'. How does Bishop help us to imagine this fish?

2 Would you agree that the images the poet uses are unusual and striking? What impression of the fish do they give us? Look in particular at the wallpaper and flower imagery.

3 Are we also given another view of the fish, in lines 16–33? How did you respond to this picture of the fish?

4 How does the poet present the fish as having human characteristics?

5 Where in the poem, however, are we made aware that this is an illusion?

6 Where would you place the moment of vision in the poem, when the poet really comes to recognise what the fish is?

7 How do Bishop's feelings about the fish change as the poem progresses? What does this tell us about her as a person?

8 Why do you think she released the fish? Who has had the 'victory' here, in your opinion?

9 Elizabeth Bishop herself once said: 'I simply try to see things afresh'. Do you think she achieves this in 'The Fish'?

10 If you were to choose this poem for inclusion in an anthology, what reasons would you give for your choice?

FILLING STATION

Oh, but it is dirty!
—this little filling station,
oil-soaked, oil-permeated
to a disturbing, over-all
black translucency.   5
Be careful with that match!

Father wears a dirty,
oil-soaked monkey suit
that cuts him under the arms,
and several quick and saucy   10
and greasy sons assist him
(it's a family filling station),
all quite thoroughly dirty.

Do they live in the station?
It has a cement porch   15
behind the pumps, and on it
a set of crushed and grease-
impregnated wickerwork;
on the wicker sofa
a dirty dog, quite comfy.   20

Some comic books provide
the only note of color—
of certain color. They lie
upon a big dim doily
draping a taboret   25
(part of the set), beside
a big hirsute begonia.

Why the extraneous plant?
Why the taboret?
Why, oh why, the doily?   30
(Embroidered in daisy stitch
with marguerites, I think,
and heavy with gray crochet.)

Somebody embroidered the doily.
Somebody waters the plant,   35
or oils it, maybe. Somebody
arranges the rows of cans
so that they softly say:
ESSO—so—so—so
to high-strung automobiles.   40
Somebody loves us all.

GLOSSARY

3 *oil-permeated*: saturated with oil

5 *translucency*: shine

8 *monkey suit*: overalls or dungarees

10 *saucy*: cheeky

18 *impregnated*: penetrated

24 *doily*: ornamental table napkin

25 *taboret*: a low seat or stool without a back or arms

27 *hirsute*: hairy

27 *begonia*: a flowering plant

28 *extraneous*: not essential

31 *daisy stitch*: an embroidery design

32 *marguerites*: daisies

33 *crochet*: a type of knitting done with a small hook

39 *so-so-so*: as explained by Bishop herself, this is 'a phrase people used to calm and soothe horses'. It refers also to the way in which the cans are arranged

GUIDELINES

This poem is from the collection *Questions of Travel* (1965).

Everything in the filling station seems oily and dirty. The poet seems to enjoy describing the grease and grime she sees, presumably during a random stop to fill up her car. She becomes aware of the family that owns and works in the station. With characteristic Bishop curiosity about the world around her, she begins to look more closely at what she sees here. As she does in some of her poems, she asks questions about what she observes so that the description leads the reader into the realm of speculation. This enables her to see beyond the surface grime, to the very real possibility that there is in fact some kind of order or loving care that keeps the place together. Might there be a feminine, maternal presence that presides over the filling station, even if that person is not visibly present to the observer?

The recognition of a possible maternal affection in the poem takes on a certain poignancy if we consider the lack of a mother in the poet's own life. However, in this poem there is no sense of self-pity. Instead, the poem has been seen as one of Bishop's most optimistic ones.

Although the poem is straightforward in style, it has also been interpreted allegorically as a metaphor for human life. From this point of view, the filling station is seen as a microcosm of all the disorder and sordidness of the world. The efforts to adorn it can be read as a metaphor for our earthly efforts to create beauty out of ugliness and aesthetic harmony out of randomness, just as the poet herself did in 'The Bight', for example. 'Somebody loves us all' may then imply a divine perspective that oversees our efforts.

The critic Guy Rotella takes this reading further. He sees the poem as satirising a certain kind of nature poem in which nature is seen as containing a 'lesson' or moral which can be discovered by the poet. (This view of the world would have been familiar to Bishop from her reading of writers such as Emerson, Thoreau and, to an extent, Robert Frost.) Rotella suggests that the description of the filling station corresponds to the descriptive aspects of such nature poems. In such poems, details of the natural scene are revealed as part of God's eternal plan, and a unifying vision is affirmed. He suggests that Bishop's final statement is ironic:

> As a glib version of comforting resolution, a slightly mocking echo of myriad poems secure in the confidence that God inscribes the world and poets can read the text, this banality satirises closure.

Rotella does go on to qualify this rather bleak reading of the poem by accepting that there is another voice in Bishop's poem, one that interprets the details of the filling station as optimistic. He comes to the conclusion that the poem does not resolve its several voices.

QUESTIONS

1 Say how the poet elaborates on her opening exclamation: 'Oh, but it is dirty!'.

2 How would you describe the poet's attitude to the filling station? Does it change at any point?

3 What puzzles the poet about the filling station?

4 Comment on the poet's use of language in this poem.

5 Who, do you think, is the 'Somebody' referred to in the final stanza? Would you agree with the critic Guy Rotella's suggestion (mentioned in the guidelines) that it might be interpreted allegorically? Do you think the poet is being entirely serious in this poem?

6 How does the poem give the impression of someone thinking aloud?

7 In your opinion, does the poem show Bishop's ability to describe things precisely?

8 What picture of Bishop does the poem reveal to the reader? Do you find the personality revealed attractive?

9 A critic once remarked on the 'deceptive casualness' of Bishop's poems. Would you agree that this view could be applied to 'Filling Station'? Give reasons for your answer.

PADDY BUSHE

B. 1948

BIOGRAPHY

Paddy Bushe was born in Dublin in 1948. He was educated at Coláiste Mhuire and at University College, Dublin. He has lived in Australia but now lives in Waterville, Co. Kerry. Married, with two grown-up children, he has worked as a teacher and served as a local councillor in Co. Kerry. He is a regular broadcaster on arts programmes on FM3 radio. His poetry collections are *Poems with Amergin*, *Teanga*, *Counsellor* and *Digging Towards the Light*. In 1988 he was runner-up in the Patrick Kavanagh Award for Poetry, and in 1990 he won the Listowel Writer's Week Award for his poem *Sceilg*. In 2000 he was invited to read his poetry in China as part of a cultural exchange.

JASMINE

What colour is jasmine? you asked
out of the blue from your wheelchair.
And suddenly the ward was filled
with the scent of possibility, hints
of journeys to strange parts.   5

The question floored us. But the gulf
was not the colours that we couldn't name
but that we couldn't recognise the road
your question had travelled, nor sound the extent
of the blue void to which it would return.   10

The ward remade itself in a hum
of conscientious care. Outside, the usual
traffic jams. We took the long way home.
Father, jasmine is a climbing plant
whose flowers are normally white or yellow.   15

And may the fragrance of its blossoms twine
around the broken trellises of your mind.

title *Jasmine*: a shrub with very fragrant flowers.

17 *trellises*: light wooden bars used for supporting climbing plants

GUIDELINES

'Jasmine' is from the collection *Digging Towards the Light* (1994). Although the poem is a personal one, it raises questions for us about the vulnerability of the mind in old age.

The poem is set in a hospital. An elderly man, who we soon learn is the speaker's father, is sitting in his wheelchair. He suddenly asks *'What colour is jasmine?'*. The question takes the listeners by surprise, probably because it is unusual, but also because it leaves them wondering where the question comes from. What has led the old man to ask this particular question at this time? What strange routes has his mind travelled?

From the first stanza the two main images of the poem – the flower, jasmine, and the image of a journey – are intertwined. The flower image suggests beauty and delicacy, and its rich scent seems to fill the hospital ward. The image of a journey represents the way in which our minds wander, sometimes along strange paths. These lines suggest the loss of mental powers that sometimes affects the elderly, and the failure to communicate that often then happens. But the sense of mystery created by the image of travel and depth (the 'blue void', almost like the depth of space itself) gives dignity to the man's situation.

In the third and fourth stanzas the poet, returning home, reflects quietly upon this experience. He addresses his father directly, answering the question he had asked about jasmine. In the last two lines it becomes clear that for him the flower has become a metaphor for his father's fading mind. These lines are very moving and loving. The poet expresses the wish that the jasmine, with its yellow and white spring-like blossoms and sweet smell, will continue to 'twine / around the broken trellises of your mind'. The metaphor suggests hope that the old man's mind, though declining, will experience beauty and peace.

THE ATMOSPHERE OF THE POEM

Although the poet describes a situation that can be painful and disturbing, the atmosphere he creates is peaceful throughout. The image of jasmine, with its scents, colours, blossoms and tendency to climb, is associated with his father's condition in a sensitive way. The image of a journey hints at opportunities rather than decline. It is true also, of course, that the journey of life leads to death, and that flowers have their place in mourning the dead.

The poet also makes use of the senses to bring the scene to life for the reader. We can almost see and smell the flowers, hear the 'hum' in the hospital ward, and feel the blossoms that 'twine'.

QUESTIONS

1 Why do you think the father's question affected the speaker of the poem as much as it did?

2 In the first stanza the poet uses the phrase 'hints / of journeys to strange parts'. Do you think this is an important idea in the poem? How is it developed in the stanzas that follow?

3 Would you agree that the imagery in the poem appeals to our senses? Support your answer with examples.

4 What wish does the speaker express for his father in the last two lines? How did you respond to it?

5 Which of these words would best describe the feelings expressed in this poem, in your view: sad, loving, puzzled? Perhaps you would suggest another word?

6 Although the poem deals with a painful subject, do you think it is depressing or comforting to read?

7 The speaker says they 'took the long way home'. Write out a brief conversation they may have had on the journey.

JOHN DONNE

1572–1631

BIOGRAPHY

Donne (pronounced 'done'), the son of a prosperous London merchant, was one of the most learned men in an age remarkable for learned men. His learning is constantly reflected in his poetry. He spent three years at Oxford and three at Cambridge. He was a student at the Inns of Court in London, where he studied law, languages and theology from four in the morning until ten at night.

Donne was born into an age of fierce, often deadly, religiously controversy. During the long reign of Elizabeth I (1558–1603), Catholics were regarded as enemies of the State and many suffered torture, imprisonment and death for upholding their faith. Donne was brought up a Catholic. His mother was related by marriage to Sir Thomas More, the Lord Chancellor of England, who had been martyred in 1535 for refusing to acknowledge the claim of Henry VIII to be head of the English Church. Four hundred years after his death, More was declared a saint by the Catholic Church. Donne's family suffered for their religion. His brother Henry died in 1593 after being arrested for concealing a priest. When he was about thirty, Donne abandoned his Catholic faith and became an Anglican. In 1615, he was ordained to the ministry of the Church of England.

As a young man, Donne was extremely ambitious, attaching himself to influential patrons as a means of advancing his career. He travelled in Europe and took part in two naval expeditions. He became secretary to Sir Thomas Egerton, a man of great power and influence. His hopes of worldly advancement were blighted when he secretly married Anne More, Egerton's niece, in 1601. She was seventeen, he almost thirty. Her father, who was Lieutenant of the Tower of London, used his power to ruin Donne's career, compelling Egerton to dismiss him and have him imprisoned. On his release, Donne had to take legal action to be reunited with his wife. He summarised the consequences of his imprudent marriage in a rueful, witty epigram ('John Donne – Anne Donne – Undone').

During his Anglican phase, Donne was a champion of his new religion, and wrote a good deal of anti-Catholic propaganda. His literary career has two broad divisions. His memorable secular poetry (love poems, elegies and satires) belongs to the first half of his life, when he enjoyed the society of women, and was especially fond of the theatre. Almost all his poetry, even the *Holy Sonnets*, was written before his ordination in 1615. This latter event marked a new phase in his literary career. He abandoned poetry for the composition of sermons, achieving fame as one of the outstanding preachers of his time. Fragments of these sermons, divorced from their original contexts, have long been part of popular discourse (for example, 'No man is an island' and 'Never send to know for whom the bell tolls; it tolls for thee'). Donne's sermons are intensely personal, expressing remorse for past sins and, above all, his obsessive interest in his own death, which was the subject of his last sermon, preached before King Charles I. The point of the sermon was reinforced by what his first biographer called 'a decayed body and a dying face'. Death is also a major theme of his poetry.

Donne became Dean of St Paul's Cathedral in London in 1621. This promotion, as he himself put it, marked the rejection of 'the mistress of my youth, Poetry' for 'the wife of mine age, Divinity [Religion]'. The evidence suggests that Donne regarded himself as a writer of sermons rather than a poet. He published virtually nothing of his poetry and took no steps to collect or preserve it. On the other hand, he saw to it that his sermons were carefully preserved for publication. His literary contemporaries saw things differently. When his poems were published after his death, some of the principal writers of his time composed impressive tributes to his originality and his inventiveness. For over two centuries, his poetry was not highly regarded. In the eighteenth century, when elegance and grace were among the desirable features of poetry, Donne's verse was seen as awkward, primitive and inelegant, partly due to the fact that his work was available only in poor, inaccurate versions. The first good text of Donne's poems was that of Grierson (1912). Following the publication of T. S. Eliot's celebrated essay 'The Metaphysical Poets' in 1923, Donne came to be regarded as a major poet, admired above all for his unique blend of thought with feeling, his exciting use of argument and analogy, and his mastery of a lively, colloquial idiom. Donne was now valued for his wit, expressed in what became known as the metaphysical conceit, which depended for its success on the ability to discover resemblances between apparently unrelated facts and ideas. There was also the delighted recognition of his constant readiness to surprise — his use of learned ideas in support of the most daring conclusions.

The Donne revival became a cult. Some important twentieth-century poets and critics, among them Eliot and Pound, were profoundly influenced by his poetry. The daring conceit with which Eliot opens 'The Love Song of J. Alfred Prufrock' is a famous example of this influence. Donne's poetry is necessarily élitist; given his tendency to exploit his massive, wide ranging store of knowledge (much of which is now obsolete or obscure) as the material of his poems. Donne appeals to the intelligence and knowledge of his readers, as well as to their imaginations. An appreciation of his poems depends ultimately on our ability to work at them in order to discover what their astonishingly broad range of reference meant to their author, and what it can mean almost four centuries later.

SONG: GOE AND CATCHE A FALLING STARRE

Goe, and catche a falling starre,
    Get with child a mandrake roote,
Tell me, where all past yeares are,
    Or who cleft the Divels foot,
Teach me to heare Mermaides singing,   5
    Or to keep off envies stinging,
        And finde
        What winde
Serves to advance an honest minde.

If thou beest borne to strange sights   10
    Things invisible to see,
Ride ten thousand daies and nights,
    Till age snow white haires on thee,
Thou, when thou retorn'st, wilt tell mee
All strange wonders that befell thee,   15
        And sweare
        No where
Lives a woman true, and faire.

If thou findst one, let mee know,
    Such a Pilgrimage were sweet;   20
Yet doe not, I would not goe,
    Though at next doore wee might meet,
Though shee were true, when you met her,
And last, till you write your letter,
        Yet shee   25
        Will bee
False, ere I come, to two, or three.

GLOSSARY

1–9 *Goe … minde*: the speaker lists a number of impossible tasks

2 *Get … root*: make a mandrake root pregnant. The mandrake, a plant with forked roots, was believed to have human qualities

4 *Who cleft the Divels foot*: the devil was said to have a cloven hoof

12 *Ride … nights*: this recalls the story of a squire who engaged in a three-year countrywide search for a chaste woman, and eventually found one: a plain countrywoman, whom he could not corrupt

18 *Lives a woman true, and faire*: the most unlikely of all discoveries would be a woman who was faithful as well as beautiful

20 *were*: would be

21 *doe not*: do not tell me

23–7 *Though … or three*: the pilgrim might find a beautiful woman who was faithful when he met her. However, by the time the speaker reached her in response to this news, she would have been unfaithful to two or three men

GUIDELINES

The theme of this witty, extravagant poem is the infidelity of women, particularly beautiful women. It is, the argument of the poem goes, as hard to find a beautiful woman who is at the same time faithful and chaste as it is to perform traditionally impossible tasks.

This is a conventionally cynical poem. The speaker rejects the possibility that a woman can be both chaste and beautiful ('true, and faire'). To make his point, he considers a number of other supposed impossibilities. The logic of the poem is that the discovery of a beautiful yet chaste woman is likely to prove as difficult as the solution to a number of notoriously impossible tasks. These are: catching a falling star; causing a mandrake root to become pregnant; discovering what has become of all the years that have passed since creation; discovering the identity of the person who caused the Devil's foot to be cloven; learning to hear the songs of mermaids; finding a method of making people secure against the envy of others, and identifying a wind that will blow good fortune to an honest person.

Having listed these impossibilities in the first stanza, the speaker spends the next two dismissing the notion that a woman both beautiful and chaste is to be found anywhere. In Stanza 2 he imagines an acquaintance going on a magical journey through the world, lasting 'ten thousand days and nights' and returning to swear that nowhere was there to be found 'a woman true, and fair'. On the other hand, as Stanza 3 suggests, perhaps the adventurer will return to reveal to the speaker that a woman both beautiful and fair does, after all, exist. This possibility gives rise to the moving reflection that the discovery of such a woman would make the 'pilgrimage' leading to her identification a 'sweet' and worthwhile event, like the revelation of some saint, whose rare combination of chastity and beauty made her remarkable.

The speaker finds it impossible to maintain his faith in the existence of such a creature and lapses into cynicism. The woman reported by the pilgrim might have been both chaste and beautiful when he met her, but it will be futile for the speaker to go in quest of her. By the time of his arrival, she would have lost her honour 'to two, or three' men.

This is one of Donne's typically witty poems. It is not simple in mood or tone. It is possible to read it as an irresponsibly flippant comment on female virtue. It may also be read as a cynical exercise based on personal experience of disillusionment or disappointment. It should be borne in mind that even Donne's most seemingly trifling poems can have serious implications, as the line 'Such a Pilgrimage were sweet' may suggest.

QUESTIONS

1 Does the speaker really believe the argument he is advancing in this poem?
2 What is the mood of the poem: is the speaker being cynical, sad, pessimistic, lighthearted or satirical for example? Or can he be serious?
3 What does the poem tell you about the kind of person the speaker is?
4 What is the significance of the reference to 'a Pilgrimage' in line 20?
5 Contrast the ideas and attitudes of this poem with those of 'The Dreame', 'The Sunne Rising', 'The Anniversarie' and the other 'Song' ('Sweetest love I do not goe').
6 The poem contains some unusual images. Comment on two of these and say what purpose they serve in the poem.
7 The poem is based on an attempt to prove a point. What is this point, and how does the poet go about proving it? Do you think he succeeds?
8 'This poem shows Donne's quickness of mind.' Comment on this idea.

THE FLEA

Marke but this flea, and marke in this,
How little that which thou deny'st me is;
It suck'd me first, and now sucks thee,
And in this flea, our two bloods mingled bee;
Thou know'st that this cannot be said   5
A sinne, nor shame, nor losse of maidenhead,
    Yet this enjoyes before it wooe,
    And pamper'd swells with one blood made of two,
    And this, alas, is more than wee would doe.

Oh stay, three lives in one flea spare,   10
Where wee almost, yea more than maryed are.
This flea is you and I, and this
Our mariage bed, and mariage temple is;
Though parents grudge, and you, w'are met,
And cloysterd in these living walls of Jet,   15
    Though use make you apt to kill mee,
    Let not to that, selfe murder added bee,
    And sacrilege, three sinnes in killing three.

Cruell and sodaine, hast thou since
Purpled thy naile, in blood of innocence?   20
Wherein could this flea guilty bee,
Except in that drop which it suckt from thee?
Yet thou triumph'st, and saist that thou
Find'st not thy selfe, nor mee the weaker now;
    'Tis true, then learne how false, feares bee;   25
    Just so much honor, when thou yeeld'st to mee,
    Will wast, as this flea's death tooke life from thee.

 5 *said*: called

 6 *maidenhead*: virginity

 9 *more … doe*: they don't want a pregnancy

10 *stay … spare*: refrain from killing the flea, and so spare three lives all at once (the flea's, yours and mine). Since their 'two bloods' are mingled in the flea because it bit both of them, he imagines both their lives present in its body

11 *maryed*: married

15 *cloysterd … Jet*: lodged inside the walls of the flea's black body

16 *use*: habit

17–18 *Let not … three*: don't add suicide and sacrilege to murder. She will be guilty of sacrilege if, by killing the flea, she destroys the temple in which they were married

19 *sodaine*: sudden, impulsive
    since: already

20 *Purpled thy naile*: she has crushed the flea to death with her nails

21 *Wherein*: in what way

25–7 *then learne … thee*: she will lose no more of her honour by yielding to him than the flea took from her when he sucked her blood

GUIDELINES

Flea poems were very common in European Renaissance literature. They were generally indecent. Here Donne deflects attention from the woman's body and focuses instead on the body of the flea. By sucking the speaker's blood and then that of his mistress, the flea becomes a symbol of the union he desires with her. Donne displays extraordinary ingenuity and skill in his witty exploration in the implications of a fleabite.

Donne organises his poem, which is a series of ingenious arguments addressed to the speaker's mistress, in three stages, each based on a nine-line stanza. In the first, he draws a moral or lesson from the flea and tries to incite his mistress to follow its example. By biting both of them and thus mingling their bloods, the flea allows the speaker to use it as an image of the physical union of a man and a woman, something he would like to enjoy with his mistress. He envies the flea who, as he fancifully imagines, can enjoy 'before it wooe'.

In the second stanza, as the woman prepares to kill the flea which has just bitten her, he warns her of the consequences of doing this. The argument of this stanza is wonderfully ingenious and, if we accept its astonishing premise, perfectly logical. It is founded on the notion that once the flea has bitten both the speaker and his mistress, it now incorporates three lives: his, hers and its own. Since their bloods are mingled in its body, within its 'living walls of Jet', the flea has been transformed into their marriage bed and their marriage temple or church, where they are united as one. The speaker uses the presence of their mingled bloods in the flea's body to arrive at the outrageous conclusion that this makes the flea their place of residence. From this he wittily, and equally outrageously, deduces that 'This flea is you and I' (line 12). This allows him to propose a further argument. If his mistress kills the flea, she will be guilty of three major offences. Firstly, she will be committing murder, by killing him inside the flea; by killing herself inside it, she will be committing suicide, and thirdly, by destroying the flea she will at the same time be destroying the temple in which they were married, and so committing sacrilege.

As the third stanza makes immediately clear, the speaker's attempts to save the flea's life are futile. The woman has killed it and so shed innocent blood. Donne's speaker extracts what advantage he can from the woman's argument that neither he nor she has suffered from what she has done to the flea. From this, he draws the odd conclusion that if she yields to him, she will lose no more honour than she did when 'this flea's death took life' from her (line 27).

J. B. Leishman remarks that:

> it is the very triviality of the subject which makes the triumph of Donne's wit so astonishing; he has performed a kind of miracle, has almost succeeded in triumphing over the laws of nature — has, as it were, made a fire without sticks, built a house without bricks, created something out of nothing, or next to nothing.

QUESTIONS

1 Here the flea appears in a variety of guises. List these. How appropriate are they to Donne's theme?

2 What is Donne trying to achieve in the poem?

3 Discuss 'The Flea' as an example of Donne's astonishing ingenuity and verbal dexterity.

4 Is the flea the central character of this poem?

5 Discuss this poem as an exercise in imagination.

6 The poem features some impressive images. Select two of these and comment on their effect.

7 The themes of guilt and innocence are central to the poem. Discuss the poet's use of these themes.

CAROL ANN DUFFY

B. 1955

BIOGRAPHY

Carol Ann Duffy was born in Glasgow in December 1955. She grew up in Staffordshire where she was educated at Stafford Girls' High School. She studied philosophy at university in Liverpool before moving to London to work as a freelance writer. She has written plays as well as poems, edited books of poetry and been a writer-in-residence at the Southern Arts, Thamesdown. She has lived in Manchester where she lectured in poetry at Manchester Metropolitan University.

Duffy has published several volumes of poems, among them *Standing Female Nude* (1985), *Selling Manhattan* (1987), *The Other Country* (1990) and *Mean Time* (1993). In 2000 she published *The World's Wife*, a collection of dramatic monologues in the voices of the wives of famous men (Mrs Midas and Mrs Aesop, for example). She has edited two anthologies for teenagers, *I Wouldn't Thank You for a Valentine* and *Stopping for Death*.

Carol Ann Duffy has been awarded many prizes for her work, among them the Forward Poetry Prize and the Whitbread Poetry Award. In 1995 she was awarded an OBE in the Queen's Birthday Honours List. She is one of the most popular women poets writing today.

VALENTINE

Not a red rose or a satin heart.

I give you an onion.
It is a moon wrapped in brown paper.
It promises light
like the careful undressing of love.   5

Here.
It will blind you with tears
like a lover.
It will make your reflection
a wobbling photo of grief.   10

I am trying to be truthful.

Not a cute card or a kissogram.

I give you an onion.
Its fierce kiss will stay on your lips,
possessive and faithful   15
as we are,
for as long as we are.

Take it.
Its platinum loops shrink to a wedding-ring,
if you like.   20

Lethal.
Its scent will cling to your fingers,
cling to your knife.

GUIDELINES

'Valentine' is from the collection *Mean Time* (1993). Like a traditional valentine, the poem contains a proposal of marriage. But unlike a traditional valentine, the proposal is expressed in unromantic terms.

The title prepares us for a romantic love poem, but what we find is rather different. Instead of the usual sorts of gifts like red roses and satin hearts, the lover gives her beloved an onion.

The speaker makes a case for the onion as an appropriate gift. The metaphors are unusual, in that ordinary things (brown paper) are mixed with romantic images (the moon). This mixture of ordinary and romantic continues through the poem and gives it its ironic, bittersweet tone, so that we are never quite sure what exactly the feelings of the speaker are. For instance, the speaker never allows us to forget that the gift is an onion, so that we find references to its layers of skin, its colour, the fact that peeling onions makes us cry, and yet each of these aspects is made to fit the speaker's view of love: that it is sexual, that it offers light and happiness, but that it can also make you cry.

The speaker thinks that an onion is a more 'truthful' symbol of love than any other more conventional Valentine's Day gift. She reveals even more clearly what she thinks love is. The smell and taste of the onion, its 'fierce kiss', will last on the lips of the beloved, just as the speaker's love will last – as long as the love they share will last. Here she seems to recognise that love may not last forever, another more honest view of love than is usually found in a valentine.

There is a sense that the speaker is appealing to her beloved – 'Take it' – as she reveals another aspect of the onion that makes it appropriate. Its white rings, as it is cut up, may become 'platinum hoops' like a wedding ring, as the speaker says rather uncertainly 'if you like'. It is as if she is not totally confident about the relationship, so that the proposal comes across as rather off-hand and casual.

You can read the final three lines in a number of ways. 'Lethal' might suggest the fierceness of love, but it has underlying suggestions of destruction. And is there a threatening tone in the image of the onion's scent that 'clings'? 'Knife' is a strange word to finish with in a poem about love. Does it have suggestions of bitterness and betrayal?

How we respond to the poem may depend on our own personal experience, but we cannot fail to see how original and honest it is.

QUESTIONS

1 Why, according to the poem's speaker, is the onion suitable as a gift for the beloved on Valentine's Day?

2 Which of the metaphors and similes that the poet uses do you find the most unusual and effective?

3 Do you think the relationship between the lovers in this poem is a happy one?

4 What attitude to love and relationships in general is suggested in this poem?

5 Do you find the speaker's vision of love honest, bitter, refreshing, off-putting? Perhaps you would prefer to use another word?

6 Imagine you are the person who has received the onion (and the poem) as a valentine. Write out the response you would make.

PAUL
DURCAN

B. 1944

BIOGRAPHY

Paul Durcan was born in Dublin in October 1944. He studie' st at UCD, but left without taking a degree. Later, he graduated with a BA i Archaeology and Medieval History from University College, Cork.

Durcan has published many collections of poetry, among them *The Berlin Wall Café* (1985), *Daddy, Daddy* (1990), *Crazy about Women* (1991), *Greetings to our Friends in Brazil* (1999) and *Cries of an Irish Caveman* (2001). *Daddy Daddy* won the prestigious Whitbread Prize for Poetry.

Paul Durcan has given readings of his poetry throughout Ireland and Britain and in many other parts of the world, including Russia and Brazil. His poetry readings are dramatic, entertaining occasions. He regularly broadcasts on RTÉ, reading his own work and speaking about literature.

Paul Durcan has lived in London and Barcelona as well as Dublin, where he now resides. He is one of Ireland's most well-known poets.

GOING HOME TO MAYO, WINTER, 1949

Leaving behind us the alien, foreign city of Dublin
My father drove through the night in an old Ford Anglia,
His five-year-old son in the seat beside him,
The rexine seat of red leatherette,
And a yellow moon peered in through the windscreen.   5
'Daddy, Daddy,' I cried, 'Pass out the moon,'
But no matter how hard he drove he could not pass out the moon.
Each town we passed through was another milestone
And their names were magic passwords into eternity:
Kilcock, Kinnegad, Strokestown, Elphin,   10
Tarmonbarry, Tulsk, Ballaghaderreen, Ballavarry;
Now we were in Mayo and the next stop was Turlough,
The village of Turlough in the heartland of Mayo,
And my father's mother's house, all oil-lamps and women,
And my bedroom over the public bar below,   15
And in the morning cattle-cries and cock-crows:
Life's seemingly seamless garment gorgeously rent
By their screeches and bellowings. And in the evenings
I walked with my father in the high grass down by the river
Talking with him – an unheard-of thing in the city.   20

But home was not home and the moon could be no more outflanked
Than the daylight nightmare of Dublin city:
Back down along the canal we chugged into the city
And each lock-gate tolled our mutual doom;
And railings and palings and asphalt and traffic-lights,   25
And blocks after blocks of so-called 'new' tenements –
Thousands of crosses of loneliness planted
In the narrowing grave of the life of the father;
In the wide, wide cemetery of the boy's childhood.

GLOSSARY

2 *Ford Anglia*: a brand of car

4 *rexine*: artificial leather used in upholstery

10 *Kilcock …Elphin*: Kilcock is in Co. Kildare; Kinnegad is in Co. Westmeath; Strokestown and Elphin are in Co. Roscommon

11 *Tarmonbarry, Tulsk, Ballaghaderreen, Ballavarry*: Co. Roscommon

12 *Turlough*: village in Co. Mayo, the birthplace of Paul Durcan's father

17 *rent*: torn

21 *outflanked*: passed out

24 *lock-gate*: gate for opening or closing a lock in a canal

25 *palings*: fences

25 *asphalt*: paving

26 *tenements*: houses divided into flats

GUIDELINES

Paul Durcan's parents came from Co. Mayo, where he spent many happy summer holidays as a child. In this poem he looks back to his childhood experience of travelling to Mayo with his father and his feelings about being there and returning to Dublin. Durcan's father was a circuit court judge, with whom the poet later had a rather troubled relationship.

From the beginning the speaker seems to see Dublin as an 'alien, foreign' place, possibly echoing his father's view of it (as a Mayoman). He describes the excitement of travelling in the car as a child, the childish desire to 'Pass out the moon', the sense of 'magic' as he names the towns through which they passed.

Vivid images of what he saw and heard bring to life his experience of actually being in Mayo on his holidays. Repetition of 'and' echoes his childish excitement. But there is a certain sadness in the image that ends the first stanza: he and his father, talking together, relax in a way that would not have happened in Dublin.

The atmosphere of the second stanza contrasts utterly with the first. Whereas life in Mayo was magical, life in Dublin was a 'daylight nightmare'. As the poet and his father return home through the city we can almost feel the weight of depression descending on him. Now the images suggest a sense of being trapped (railings, palings), the blocks of new tenements or Corporation flats becoming a metaphor for a kind of death and burial, for both himself and his father. The word 'loneliness' suggests that their return marked the end of the closeness that they had in Mayo.

QUESTIONS

1 What impression do you get of the relationship between the poet and his father as they travel to Mayo?

2 Do you think the use of placenames adds to the effect of the poem? Give reasons.

3 Contrast the poet's attitude to Mayo with his attitude to Dublin. Look carefully at the poet's use of language.

4 Do you think Durcan describes his childhood experience well? Give reasons for your view.

5 How would you describe the tone of the poem? Angry? Disappointed? Nostalgic? Sad? Perhaps you would suggest another word?

6 Do you like this poem? Give reasons for your answer.

7 You want to make a short film of this poem. Describe the sort of atmosphere you would like to create, and say what music, sound effects and images you would use.

T.S. ELIOT

1888–1965

BIOGRAPHY

Thomas Stearns Eliot was born on 26 September 1888, in St Louis, Missouri. He was the youngest son of Charlotte Champe Stearns Eliot and Henry Ware Eliot. Charlotte Eliot was a clever woman who wrote poetry and encouraged her son in his literary endeavours. Henry Eliot was a businessman, president of the Hydraulic Brick Company, and a prosperous member of a Bostonian family that had distinguished itself in society.

As a child Thomas went to school in St Louis. In 1906 he entered Harvard University, taking his BA in 1909 and his MA in 1911. At first he seemed to be set on an academic career, but while he was still a student he began to write poetry. This disappointed his father who had expected him to become a Harvard Professor. Eliot then spent some years in France and Germany, studying literature and philosophy. He moved to England shortly after the outbreak of the First World War in 1914. He studied Greek philosophy at Oxford, taught at a school in London, and then obtained a position with Lloyd's Bank.

Though he returned to the United States for brief visits in later years, Eliot now settled permanently in England, becoming a British citizen in 1927.

It was in London in 1914 that Eliot met another American poet, Ezra Pound. Pound recognised the importance of the poem 'The Love Song of J. Alfred

Prufrock' (written in 1911) and arranged for its publication in the literary magazine *Poetry* in 1915. The poem was subsequently reprinted in the volume *Prufrock and other Observations* (1917). This was the collection which first introduced T. S. Eliot's poetry to a wider readership.

In 1915, after a two-month courtship, Eliot married Vivienne Haigh-Wood, an English girl from a conventional upper-middle-class family. The marriage was not a success. Vivienne's mental illness, their financial problems and personal incompatibility contributed to the extreme unhappiness they both suffered. This experience of marital unhappiness is reflected in many of Eliot's poems and particularly in his plays. It also contributed to his own physical and psychological breakdown in 1921, when he applied for leave from Lloyd's Bank and went to Lausanne to recuperate. It was in these months that he wrote the main part of *The Waste Land*, one of the most famous poems of the twentieth century.

From the 1920s onwards, Eliot became an influential literary figure. He edited *The Criterion* (to which his wife also contributed), wrote for other literary periodicals, and finally joined the publishing firm Faber and Faber in 1925. His literary criticism, collected in volumes such as the *Selected Essays* (1932) and *The Use of Poetry and the Use of Criticism* (1935), were instrumental in forming the taste of his generation. In particular he revived interest in the Metaphysical poets of the seventeenth century, such as Donne and Herbert, and in the eighteenth century poet John Dryden.

In 1927 Eliot became a member of the Anglican Church. This decision marked a momentous change in his life and his poetry. In the years following his 'conversion', he wrote a number of poems on religious themes. His personal life changed too with the decision to separate from his wife Vivienne in 1932, despite her opposition. Up until her death in a mental hospital, in 1947, she refused to accept the separation. Although his treatment of her seems callous at times, biographers have documented the disastrous effect the marriage had on both husband and wife.

During the Second World War Eliot contributed to the war effort by acting as Fire-Duty Officer during the London Blitz. At the beginning of the war in 1939 he published a collection of light verse, *Old Possum's Book of Practical Cats* (on which the musical *Cats* was based, later in the century). 'East Coker' (1940), 'Burnt Norton' (1941), 'Dry Salvages' (1941) and 'Little Gidding' (1942) were published together as *Four Quartets* in 1943. These were Eliot's last poems of any great significance.

Eliot had earlier experimented with poetic drama. *The Rock* (1934) was an ecclesiastical pageant. *Murder in the Cathedral* (1935), based on the murder of

Thomas a Becket, was a theatrically effective ritual drama. Later plays included *The Family Reunion* (1939), *The Cocktail Party* (1950), *The Confidential Clerk* (1954) and *The Elder Statesman* (1959). Although these plays achieved some critical approval at the time, later generations have not acclaimed them to the same degree and they are seldom produced in the commercial theatre.

In 1948 T. S. Eliot received the Nobel Prize for Literature in recognition of his achievements and status as poet and critic. He continued to write literary and cultural criticism, including *Notes Towards the Definition of Culture* (1948) and *On Poetry and Poets* (1957). He was much in demand as lecturer and visiting poet. His *Collected Plays* appeared in 1962. *Collected Poems 1909–1962* was published in 1963. At the age of 68, to the surprise of his friends and family, he married his secretary, Valerie Fletcher, a woman thirty years his junior. This marriage brought him great contentment, despite the ill-health he suffered as he grew older.

He died on 4 January 1965. His remains are buried in East Coker, the village in Somerset from where his family had emigrated to America in the seventeenth century.

PRELUDES

I
The winter evening settles down
With smell of steaks in passageways.
Six o'clock.
The burnt-out ends of smoky days.
And now a gusty shower wraps   5
The grimy scraps
Of withered leaves about your feet
And newspapers from vacant lots;
The showers beat
On broken blinds and chimney-pots,   10
And at the corner of the street
A lonely cab-horse steams and stamps.

And then the lighting of the lamps.

II
The morning comes to consciousness
Of faint stale smells of beer   15
From the sawdust-trampled street
With all its muddy feet that press
To early coffee-stands.
With the other masquerades
That time resumes,   20
One thinks of all the hands
That are raising dingy shades
In a thousand furnished rooms.

III

You tossed a blanket from the bed,
You lay upon your back, and waited;   25
You dozed, and watched the night revealing
The thousand sordid images
Of which your soul was constituted;
They flickered against the ceiling.
And when all the world came back   30
And the light crept up between the shutters,
And you heard the sparrows in the gutters,
You had such a vision of the street
As the street hardly understands;
Sitting along the bed's edge, where   35
You curled the papers from your hair,
Or clasped the yellow soles of feet
In the palms of both soiled hands.

IV

His soul stretched tight across the skies
That fade behind a city block,   40
Or trampled by insistent feet
At four and five and six o'clock;
And short square fingers stuffing pipes,
And evening newspapers, and eyes
Assured of certain certainties,   45
The conscience of a blackened street
Impatient to assume the world.

I am moved by fancies that are curled
Around these images, and cling:
The notion of some infinitely gentle   50
Infinitely suffering thing.

Wipe your hand across your mouth, and laugh;
The worlds revolve like ancient women
Gathering fuel in vacant lots.

GLOSSARY

title *Preludes*: a prelude is a short, introductory piece of music

8 *vacant lots*: empty building sites

19 *masquerades*: disguises, false pretences

36 *curled the papers*: paper was once used to curl hair

GUIDELINES

'Preludes' is from the collection *Prufrock and Other Observations* (1917). Like many of Eliot's poems, it was not written as a complete work. The first two preludes were written when Eliot was at Harvard in 1909–10. The third prelude was written a year later in Paris, the fourth at Harvard in 1911–12.

The imagery of the scenes described in 'Preludes' shows Eliot's sense of how squalid and sordid urban life can be. At the time of writing, he was reading the novels of Charles-Louis Philippe, who depicted the city as a degrading place. Eliot remarked in later years that the urban imagery was that of St Louis (his birthplace), Boston, London and Paris.

The title suggests an analogy with music. A prelude is an introduction to a piece of music. Preludes often create mood pictures on a certain theme, making use of repetition and variation to create atmosphere. Eliot's poem follows this musical pattern. The title also sets up an ironic contrast between the lyricism suggested by the musical analogy and the unpleasant nature of the city landscape.

PRELUDE 1

Ideas, images and even phrases are repeated throughout the four preludes. The evening setting which opens the poem is echoed by the setting of the last prelude, giving the poem a symmetrical shape. Each prelude presents the world of the city from a different perspective. This creates what many critics have called a cinematic effect.

Eliot makes use of many poetic devices from the beginning. Rich sensuous images evoke the winter evening in the first prelude. Vivid adjectives and sound effects play their part in evoking a bleak atmosphere. The last line relieves the dreary mood somewhat, but hardly enough to make up for what has gone before.

PRELUDE 2

The second prelude describes a morning scene, but the mood is still bleak. The 'consciousness' that registers the scene is kept deliberately vague and impersonal.

The invisible observer seems to suggest that all experience is a masquerade, something false and deceptive. The 'hands ... raising dingy shades' (blinds) may be seen as people raising a curtain to reveal their lives, as in a theatre. This is an image that reinforces the idea of the artificial, unreal life of those who live in the city. The overall mood, as in the first prelude, is weary and depressed.

PRELUDE 3

In the third prelude we view this urban landscape more specifically from the perception of a woman. She is a passive observer of her world, sluggishly registering the ugliness of the street. In creating the image of the soul as made of a 'thousand sordid images', Eliot was influenced by the ideas of the French philosopher, Henri Bergson. He propounded the idea that the soul was formed by the memory of images projected into the passive mind, as in a film. (We are reminded of Prufrock's 'magic lantern'.) This woman is depicted in images that limit her to parts of her body only, depersonalising her and symbolising the squalid life she leads.

PRELUDE 4

In the fourth prelude an anonymous man depicts the city in images that are just as unattractive as those perceived by the woman. He too has been affected by his surroundings, so much so that his very soul has been destroyed. This is an image of his complete spiritual and psychological suffering. Time has passed, so that it is evening, as in the first prelude.

There is another speaker in the poem, the 'I' of lines 48–51. This speaker seems to have a longing for a different kind of existence, one that goes beyond the surface meaninglessness of life. He feels for a moment the almost palpable presence of something that is not there (it is a 'notion' merely.) What this 'infinitely gentle / Infinitely suffering thing' may be is left deliberately vague, but it hints at a sense of goodness that redeems the essentially bleak vision of the poem. It is as if the desolate nature of the city may have still a value beyond what its surface suggests. (Eliot was always fascinated by ideas of appearance and reality and the discrepancy between them.)

However, the last three lines present us with a negative image that causes the more positive intuition to evaporate cruelly, as the poet's tentative vision is discarded with a dismissive gesture and a mocking laugh. The final image is one of utter desolation. It suggests an acceptance of a universe that is indifferent to us and our human feelings.

QUESTIONS

1 Would you agree that the images of evening in Part I of 'Preludes' are remarkably vivid and sensuous?

2 What is the dominant atmosphere created in Part II of 'Preludes'? Say how the language used conveys the mood here.

3 A character is introduced in Part III of 'Preludes'. What sort of lifestyle is presented? How did you respond to the description?

4 The images and metaphors in Part IV introduce a spiritual note. What do they symbolise? Look at the connotations of words such as 'trampled', 'conscience', 'blackened'.

5 Would you agree that the speaker of the poem, the 'I' of Part IV, is reaching out for an entirely different way of life from the one depicted throughout the poem? In what tone is this idea expressed?

6 How do the last three lines affect our reading of the poem?

7 The poet Stephen Spender thought that 'Preludes' represented some of Eliot's finest work. Would you agree with this view?

8 You have been asked to compile an anthology to include three of Eliot's poems. You choose 'Preludes' as one of them. Write out the case you would make for your choice.

AUNT HELEN

Miss Helen Slingsby was my maiden aunt,
And lived in a small house near a fashionable square
Cared for by servants to the number of four.
Now when she died there was silence in heaven
And silence at her end of the street.   5
The shutters were drawn and the undertaker wiped his feet—
He was aware that this sort of thing had occurred before.
The dogs were handsomely provided for,
But shortly afterwards the parrot died too.
The Dresden clock continued ticking on the mantlepiece,   10
And the footman sat upon the dining-table
Holding the second housemaid on his knees—
Who had always been so careful while her mistress lived.

GLOSSARY

10 *Dresden clock*: a fine china clock made in Dresden, Germany.

GUIDELINES

'Aunt Helen' was included in the volume *Prufrock and Other Observations*, published in 1917. It is one of a number of poems in which Eliot commented on (or 'observed') the manners and society of his native Boston, New England.

'Aunt Helen' is a satirical portrait of a type of woman whom Eliot would have known very well in his youth. At that time, life in upper-class Boston society was rigidly conventional, almost stultifying. The poem makes its impact because of the contrasts it creates between the respectable way of life of Aunt Helen and the underlying forces of sexuality and disorder that she has succeeded in repressing by her personality.

Aunt Helen's lifestyle is fixed for us in a few well-chosen images that suggest a genteel, well-to-do but not showy woman. The speaker, her nephew, expresses no feelings of regret. Calling his aunt 'Miss Helen Slingsby' hints at the formality of their relationship. Reactions to her death are conventional at best, as the ironic tone conveys.

The details that follow in the poem underline the emptiness of Aunt Helen's life. There is no reference to any human beings who were of concern to her (even her nephew). However, she saw to it that her dogs were looked after. We could interpret the death of the parrot in a number of ways: was he the only creature that felt any grief? Or is the speaker suggesting that both their deaths were of equal (non-) significance, especially since the 'Dresden clock continued ticking'?

The last three lines pull us up with images of sexuality that contrast sharply with the order and decorum of Aunt Helen's life as a maiden aunt. It is as if the footman and the housemaid have been released from a kind of slavery to convention that ruled the household and are now free to behave as they wish.

Although the poem is satirical in tone, it avoids being judgmental and instead makes its effect through gentle irony.

QUESTIONS

1 What impression of Miss Helen Slingsby's life is given in the first three lines of the poem? What would you say the poet's attitude is to this way of life? How can we tell?

2 What do you think the line 'Now when she died there was silence in heaven' suggests? Is the poet being ironic here, in view of the way Aunt Helen lived her life?

3 How do you respond to the description of the undertaker's reaction to her death?

4 Why do you think the poet mentions the dogs, the parrot and the Dresden clock?

5 Explore the image of the footman and the housemaid carefully. Do you find it amusing, unexpected, revealing or rather shocking in the context of the poem? What might it suggest about the values underlying the society in which Aunt Helen lived?

6 Would you agree that what the poem leaves unsaid is almost as important as what it says?

7 Would you agree that the language used in the poem suits the poem's theme very well?

ROBERT FROST

1874–1963

BIOGRAPHY

Robert Frost was born in San Francisco in 1874. At the age of eleven, following the death of his father, Frost moved with his family to New England. He attended Dartmouth College but failed to finish his undergraduate course, taking a job at a mill instead. He started to study again in 1897 at Harvard University, but left without taking a degree. He tried shoemaking, teaching, editing a local paper and then farming. In 1895 he married Elinor White, to whom he was married for forty-three years. They had six children, one of whom died in infancy. For a number of years the family lived on a farm which Frost had inherited from his grandfather. He also supplemented his income by teaching, which he enjoyed. However in 1911 Frost sold the farm and moved to England, where he hoped to find literary success.

His first book of poems, *A Boy's Will*, was published in England in 1913. His originality was recognised by leading poet and fellow American Ezra Pound, who praised Frost for having 'the good sense to speak naturally and to paint the thing, the thing as he sees it'. W. B. Yeats, too, called the volume 'the best poetry written in America for a long time'.

Frost now began to enjoy the friendship and acceptance of the English literary society of the time. His second collection, *North of Boston* (1914), received excellent reviews.

Having returned to America in 1915, frost and his family settled on a farm in New Hampshire. The life of a farmer appealed to him. His experience of rural life is reflected in his third collection, *Mountain Interval* (1916), in which several of his most famous lyrics appear.

His life now combined farming, family life, writing and lecturing. This was very much the pattern that would continue for the rest of his life. He was a gifted speaker, with his mixture of homespun Yankee wisdom, poetic insights and sense of humour. Invitations to speak and read his poems around the country poured in. The collection *New Hampshire* (1923) consolidated his already formidable reputation, and in 1924 he was awarded the first of four Pulitzer Prizes for Poetry which he won during his lifetime, a record number for any poet. *West-Running Brook* (1928) was followed by the *Collected Poems* in 1931. In the same year he was elected to the American Academy of Arts and Letters. Many honorary degrees and public awards followed. His other published collections were *A Further Range* (1936), *A Witness Tree* (1942), *Steeple Bush* (1947) and his last collection, *In the Clearing* (1962).

Frost's public success was not mirrored by his personal life. He himself suffered from depression. One of his daughters died at the age of twenty-nine. His wife Elinor died in 1938. His only son committed suicide in 1940. Although Frost does not refer directly to these events, it may be that the trauma of these experiences is reflected in the occasional darkness of his poems.

Robert Frost died in 1963 at the age of 89.

THE ROAD NOT TAKEN

Two roads diverged in a yellow wood,
And sorry I could not travel both
And be one traveler, long I stood
And looked down one as far as I could
To where it bent in the undergrowth;   5

Then took the other, as just as fair,
And having perhaps the better claim,
Because it was grassy and wanted wear;
Though as for that, the passing there
Had worn them really about the same,   10

And both that morning equally lay
In leaves no step had trodden black.
Oh, I kept the first for another day!
Yet knowing how way leads on to way,
I doubted if I should ever come back.   15

I shall be telling this with a sigh
Somewhere ages and ages hence:
Two roads diverged in a wood, and I—
I took the one less traveled by,
And that has made all the difference.   20

GUIDELINES

'The Road Not Taken' is from *Mountain Interval* (1916). It is said to have been inspired by Frost's friend, the poet Edward Thomas, whom he had met in England and who was subsequently killed in the First World War. Thomas was apparently in the habit of expressing regret at whatever decision he had taken.

The poem dramatises the choices we are presented with in life and their consequences. The poet uses the metaphor of two roads, one of which he had to take. He then reflects on the choice he made. Not only does he review the reasons for his decision, such as they were, but he visualises himself examining it at some time in the future.

The poem is one of Robert Frost's most popular and often-quoted poems, no doubt because it deals with a universal theme. A number of interpretations have been put forward. Is the poem concerned with choice of career in life? (We may remember that Robert Frost himself left his life as a farmer in New England to develop his gifts as a poet.) Or does the poem hint at a moral struggle that has to be confronted, in which the least popular and most difficult option is chosen? And how do we interpret the last lines of the poem?

The setting of the poem is extremely attractive, with the 'yellow wood' evoking the famous New England fall. As in many of Frost's poems, images of nature are described not merely for their own sake, but to suggest an analogy with human concerns.

QUESTIONS

1 How are the 'two roads' presented, as they appeared to the speaker?
2 Can you trace the speaker's train of thought as he makes his decision?
3 Do you think the speaker is happy with his decision? How can we tell from the tone of the poem? Look especially at the last stanza.
4 Can you speculate about the choices in Frost's life (or anyone else's) that may be symbolised in this poem?
5 What do you think the poet means by the final line: 'And that has made all the difference'?
6 Can you understand why this is a well-loved poem in America and elsewhere?

"OUT, OUT—"

The buzz saw snarled and rattled in the yard
And made dust and dropped stove-length sticks of wood,
Sweet-scented stuff when the breeze drew across it.
And from there those that lifted eyes could count
Five mountain ranges one behind the other   5
Under the sunset far into Vermont.
And the saw snarled and rattled, snarled and rattled,
As it ran light, or had to bear a load.
And nothing happened: day was all but done.
Call it a day, I wish they might have said   10
To please the boy by giving him the half hour
That a boy counts so much when saved from work.
His sister stood beside them in her apron
To tell them "Supper." At the word, the saw,
As if to prove saws knew what supper meant,   15
Leaped out of the boy's hand, or seemed to leap—
He must have given the hand. However it was,
Neither refused the meeting. But the hand!
The boy's first outcry was a rueful laugh,
As he swung toward them holding up the hand,   20
Half in appeal, but half as if to keep
The life from spilling. Then the boy saw all—
Since he was old enough to know, big boy
Doing a man's work, though a child at heart—
He saw all spoiled. "Don't let him cut my hand off—   25
The doctor, when he comes. Don't let him, sister!"
So. But the hand was gone already.
The doctor put him in the dark of ether.
He lay and puffed his lips out with his breath.
And then—the watcher at his pulse took fright.   30
No one believed. They listened at his heart.
Little—less—nothing!—and that ended it.
No more to build on there. And they, since they
Were not the one dead, turned to their affairs.

GLOSSARY

title *"Out, out—"*: the title alludes to Shakespeare's lines in the tragedy, Macbeth. The line is 'Out, Out, brief candle!' when Macbeth himself speaks of the brevity and sadness of life

6 *Vermont*: a state in New England, USA

GUIDELINES

'Out, Out—' is from the collection *Mountain Interval* (1916). One of Robert Frost's most affecting poems, it is based on a true story. In 1910 the child of one of Frost's neighbours in Vermont, New England, died as a result of an accident on his father's farm. The local newspaper, *The Littleton Courier*, reported the incident like this:

> *Raymond Tracy Fitzgerald, one of the twin sons of Michael G. and Margaret Fitzgerald of Bethlehem, died at his home Thursday afternoon, March 24, as a result of an accident by which one of his hands was badly hurt in a sawing machine. The young man was assisting in sawing up some wood in his own dooryard with a sawing machine and accidentally hit the loose pulley, causing the saw to descend upon his hand, cutting and lacerating it very badly. Raymond was taken into the house and a physician was immediately summoned, but he died very suddenly from the effects of shock, which produced heart failure.*

Frost's narrative poem dramatises the incident reported above. The scene is set in the yard of the New England farm. From the beginning, the saw seems to be almost like another character in the drama, personified by 'snarled', with ominous implications. Without direct comment, the poem conveys a great deal about the hardworking and possibly even harsh conditions in which the boy lives and ultimately dies, adding to the sense of impending doom as the poem proceeds.

Critics have paid attention to the strangeness of the image of the saw as an animate object seemingly looking on the boy's hand as its 'supper'. And the line that follows almost goes so far as to suggest that the boy willed his death, or at least did nothing to prevent it.

But it is the depiction of the boy's death itself that has attracted most comment. The boy knows he is facing death: 'He saw all spoiled'. The word 'spoiled' suggests simply that the boy's future is spoiled, as of course it is. Frost's biographer Jay Parini interprets 'spoiled' as referring to the family dynamic that is now altered for ever:

The boy has subliminally come to understand that within the framework of a subsistence economy there is small room for a boy who cannot pull his weight. Circumstances are such that an extra 'hand' is essential for survival.

Such a reading, although harsh, fits in with the tone of the concluding lines of the poem.

The boy's death is described with no expression of grief or consolatory comment. But it is the reaction of those who are still living that takes us aback: 'And they, since they / Were not the one dead, turned to their affairs'.

QUESTIONS

1 Would you agree that there is a sense of foreboding in the poem from the beginning? How is this sense created?

2 What impression of rural life is given in the poem? How did you respond to it?

3 Are there any particular lines in the poem that puzzled or disturbed you? Can you say why?

4 What might the poet be suggesting in the line beginning 'Then the boy saw all …'?

5 Examine the last two lines of the poem. Do you think this is an appropriate way to respond to a tragic death such as this? Do you find the effect chilling, callous, resigned, accepting, realistic? Perhaps your response could be described in an entirely different way? You might link your response with the impression of rural life you got from reading the entire poem.

6 Would you agree that this is a dramatic poem? Take into account the setting, characters, climax and ending, as well as the poem's title.

7 Do you like this poem?

ACQUAINTED WITH THE NIGHT

I have been one acquainted with the night.
I have walked out in rain—and back in rain.
I have outwalked the furthest city light.

I have looked down the saddest city lane.
I have passed by the watchman on his beat   5
And dropped my eyes, unwilling to explain.

I have stood still and stopped the sound of feet
When far away an interrupted cry
Came over houses from another street,

But not to call me back or say good-by;   10
And further still at an unearthly height
One luminary clock against the sky

Proclaimed the time was neither wrong nor right.
I have been one acquainted with the night.

GLOSSARY

12 *luminary clock*: a clock that gives out light (possibly the moon)

GUIDELINES

This short lyric, a sonnet, is from *West-Running Brook* (1928). The poem is unusual among Frost's work in that it is set in the city rather than in rural surroundings. It depicts the dark, alienating side of urban existence. The speaker in the poem experiences a sense of deep depression and loneliness as he walks through the city streets.

The title of the poem and the first line set up a rich association of ideas for the reader. It seems clear that the 'night' is not meant purely literally but also reflects the 'dark night of the soul' that the speaker has experienced. Nature itself seems to echo his sadness and despair. There is a suggestion of hidden violence in the city. But what strikes the reader most perhaps is the sense of isolation that the poem expresses. It may be that the 'luminary clock' he sees (possibly the moon or an actual lit-up clock) symbolises, in a general way, the passage of time. Its message, 'the time was neither wrong nor right', is slightly mysterious. Is it saying that time is indifferent to those who live in the isolation of the city? That right or wrong is irrelevant in urban life? It may also echo Hamlet's expression of despair in Shakespeare's play: 'The time is out of joint'.

The poem is a sonnet of fourteen lines, but it is not divided into the traditional octave and sestet or three quatrains and a couplet. Instead there are four tercets (three-line stanzas) and a couplet with the rhyming pattern *aba bcb cdc ded aa*. Apart from the rhyming couplet, this rhyme pattern corresponds to what is called terza rima. The Italian poet Dante, who invented the form, wrote in his *Inferno* about a descent into hell. Frost would have had this in mind as he chose the form in which to express his own sense of despair.

Critics have pointed out that 'Acquainted with the Night' shows Robert Frost's awareness of the themes and poetic technique of modernist poets of the early twentieth century, such as T. S. Eliot and Ezra Pound, for whom the city was an image of alienation. Certainly the poem offers a contrast in the work of a poet whose social vision seems so optimistic, as expressed in 'The Tuft of Flowers' or 'Mending Wall'.

It may be that in this poem Robert Frost reveals some of his darkest fears about living – fears that were reflected in his frequent bouts of depression and psychosomatic illness during his lifetime. One of Frost's critics, Lionel Trilling, caused quite a stir when he once referred to Frost as 'a tragic poet whose work conceived of a terrifying universe'. Poems such as 'Acquainted with the Night', 'Design' and 'Provide, Provide' would bear out this perception of Frost's vision.

QUESTIONS

1 What do you think the poet suggests when he says that he has been 'acquainted with the night'? How do the images that follow develop this opening statement?

2 Would you agree that the sound of the poem echoes the poet's emotions? Look, for instance, at the rhymes used, the rhythm within the lines, the repetitions and the onomatopoeic effects of the long vowel sounds.

3 How is the indifference of the city suggested in the imagery of the poem?

4 What insight does the poem give us into Robert Frost as a person, in your opinion?

5 Do you find this poem different in tone from other poems by Frost on your course?

6 How did you respond to the theme and mood of the poem?

PATRICK KAVANAGH

1904–67

BIOGRAPHY

Patrick Kavanagh was born on October 21, 1904 in the parish of Inniskeen, in a thatched cottage built in 1791, one of ten children born to his parents, James and Bridget. Patrick attended the local Kednaminsha and Rocksavage National School until the age of fourteen, when he left it to become an apprentice shoemaker in his father's workshop. His father was an excellent musician who possessed a rich store of stories. He was a source of encouragement to Patrick. Unusually for the parish, James Kavanagh bought the newspaper on a daily basis, and this fostered his son's love of newspapers and journalism.

His mother, Bridget Quinn, was a hard-working, thrifty woman, who dreamed of owning a farm to pass on to her children. She loved Patrick, and was proud of his interest in books and writing, but she also scolded him for his daydreaming.

In 1909, the family was prosperous enough to build a new house on the site of the old, about a mile outside the village of Inniskeen. Two years later they purchased six acres of arable land and three acres of bog adjoining their holding. Patrick had three older sisters but he was the older of the two boys in the family so much of the work fell on him when the family bought a small farm holding in Shancoduff, about a half mile from their house, in 1926. When James Kavanagh died in 1929, Patrick stayed on to run the family business and work the small farm under his mother's direction, while his younger brother, Peter, went to Dublin to train as a teacher.

Kavanagh was first published in 1928 in the *Irish Weekly Independent*. He was also published in the *Irish Statesman*, where the editor was the poet and mystic Æ (George Russell), who encouraged the young poet. Kavanagh walked to Dublin to meet him and returned with an armful of books that Æ gave him.

Between 1929 and 1936, Kavanagh lived the life of a small farmer by day and a poet by night. Following the publication of his first collection of poetry in 1936, Kavanagh went to London and was contracted to write his autobiography to be called *The Green Fool* and published in 1938. However, a successful libel action was taken against it by Oliver St John Gogarty, over an innocent remark, and the book was suppressed. It was not republished until 1967. The appearance of 'The Great Hunger' in 1942, a long poem charting Kavanagh's disillusionment with Church and State and the arid poverty of the small farmer, met with a hostile reception. The 1948 autobiographical fiction *Tarry Flynn* is a gentler work, revealing Kavanagh's fondness for, and impatience with, the Monaghan of his youth and childhood. The novel charts the work, frustrations and moments of poetic insight of the young hero on a small farm in Monaghan during the 1930s. It was banned by the Censorship Board, although the ban was lifted on appeal and the novel proved quite popular.

Kavanagh moved to Dublin in 1939 where his brother, Peter, was teaching. However, the city did not provide him with the longed-for fame and recognition. There were periods of sustained energy and success, including the thirteen weeks in 1952 in which he and his brother produced *Kavanagh's Weekly*, a journal of political, social and literary comment. On the whole, though, he felt an outsider in the city. In a fit of depression he said that his move to Dublin was the greatest mistake of his life.

Kavanagh made a precarious living out of journalism and lived a hand-to-mouth existence. He wrote on all manner of subjects and was, for a number of years in the late 1940s, a film critic for *The Standard*, a Catholic weekly newspaper. Kavanagh fell in love with a number of women through the 1940s and 1950s. However, the relationships failed and the impoverished and dishevelled writer remained a bachelor until months before he died.

In Dublin Kavanagh's health suffered. In 1955 he underwent an operation for lung cancer. His excessive drinking further undermined his health. Kavanagh made many enemies in the city. He was scathing in his criticisms of other writers and his personality was thorny and complex. He was, by turns, indignant, disappointed, proud and sensitive. He was also dogged by self-doubt, self-pity and bad luck.

The year 1955 was the low point in Kavanagh's life. He was the subject of a hostile, mocking profile in *The Leader* in 1952 and sued for libel. The action was heard in 1954. The barrister acting for the paper, John A. Costello, later Taoiseach, humiliated Kavanagh. The accounts of Costello's cross-examination of the poet, published each day in the *Irish Times,* were a source of entertainment to many. Kavanagh lost the case and shortly afterwards underwent his operation for lung cancer. He was left, he said, with a 'horrible spirit of desolation', though some acquaintances suggest that Kavanagh enjoyed the role of martyr and victim.

Kavanagh characterised his recuperation from the lung cancer as a process of spiritual renewal and pointed to the canal poems as the fruits of his rebirth.

For the last eight years or so of his life, Kavanagh wrote regularly for the *Irish Farmers Journal* and the *RTÉ Guide.* This journalism provided him with a regular income. He also gave extra-mural lectures in UCD. But the advantage of regular income was offset by his heavy drinking and gambling, and he produced little poetry in these last years. There were some rewards – trips to England and America, a growing admiration of his work from a new generation of poets, and marriage to a long-time friend and lover, Katherine Barry Maloney, seven months before he died.

Kavanagh believed that he had never received the recognition he deserved. Writing an introduction to his collected poems, three years before his death, he said, 'I have never been much considered by the English critics'. Ironically, Seamus Heaney, deeply influenced by Kavanagh, is the most highly regarded poet in the English-speaking world. However, while Kavanagh complained of a lack of recognition, he also repudiated much of his own work, protesting that his worst work had been anthologised and his best ignored. This kind of protest alienated Kavanagh from those who sought to support him and it might well have been his difficult personality that worked against him gaining the recognition that his achievement deserved.

SHANCODUFF

My black hills have never seen the sun rising,
Eternally they look north towards Armagh.
Lot's wife would not be salt if she had been
Incurious as my black hills that are happy
When dawn whitens Glassdrummond chapel.   5

My hills hoard the bright shillings of March
While the sun searches in every pocket.
They are my Alps and I have climbed the Matterhorn
With a sheaf of hay for three perishing calves
In the field under the Big Forth of Rocksavage.   10

The sleety winds fondle the rushy beards of Shancoduff
While the cattle-drovers sheltering in the Featherna Bush
Look up and say: 'Who owns them hungry hills
That the water-hen and snipe must have forsaken?
A poet? Then by heavens he must be poor.'   15
I hear and is my heart not badly shaken?

GLOSSARY

title *Shancoduff*: this comes from the Irish 'Seanchua Dubh'. 'Seanchua' means 'old hollow', while 'Dubh' means 'black'. The fields in Shancoduff faced northwards and never enjoyed full sunlight

3 *Lot's wife*: in the Old Testament story, God was determined to destroy the cities of Sodom and Gomorrah. Before the destruction two angels led Lot and his family from the city, telling them not to look back. Lot's wife looked back and was turned into a pillar of salt

5 *Glassdrummond*: situated in the sunnier South Armagh

6 *hoard the bright shillings*: a shilling was a small silver coin. The line is usually read as meaning that the black hills hoard the brightness of sleet and snow after the sun has melted them on south-facing hills

8 *Matterhorn*: one of the peaks in the Alps between Switzerland and Italy

10 *Forth*: a local pronunciation of fort. The Forth of Rocksavage is an ancient hill-fort

11 *rushy*: Kavanagh described his fields at Shancoduff as 'watery'. He liked adjectives which ended in 'y' and often invented his own by adding a 'y' to a noun, as in 'sleety'

12 *cattle-drovers*: a drover was someone who herded cattle to markets, in the days before cattle-trucks. Drovers also bought and sold cattle. The work was hard and drovers had a reputation for being tough and practical

14 *snipe*: a bird with a long bill. Both the water-hen and the snipe are found in poor, marshy land. However, the land around Shancoduff is so poor that even these birds have given up on it

GUIDELINES

This poem was written in 1934, two years before Kavanagh went to London to write, and five years before he moved permanently to Dublin. In 1926 the Kavanaghs bought a small farm at Shancoduff, half a mile from the family home. Though the fields were hilly and the soil was poor, Kavanagh had a deep love for Shancoduff. Peter Kavanagh, the poet's brother says:

> *Shancoduff was more than a farm for Patrick – it was a wonderland which enriched his imagination for the rest of his life. Almost mountain-high, the fields provided a scenic view that stretched fifteen miles to the Mourne mountains.*

'Shancoduff' is a lover's presentation of his chosen place. The first word of the poem, the possessive and affectionate 'My,' sets the scene for the portrait which follows and the whole poem can be read as the lover's defence against the estimation of the land's worthlessness by those who do not love it. Shancoduff's meagre virtues are exalted and amplified. Unlike Lot's wife, Kavanagh is declaring his contentment with the provincial and the parochial. Like his beloved hills, Kavanagh sets his face against Dublin and literary society.

However, the final two lines suggest that Kavangh was conscious of the exaggeration in his description of these fields. For all his affection, the hills remain black and barren. There is an interesting ambiguity in the final two lines, an ambiguity that marks all Kavanagh's poetry on his native place. Kavanagh was caught between pride and affection for his home place and doubt as to whether it could feed his poetic imagination. It is the poet's heart which is shaken by the drover's estimation of the land. The fear is less that the land will prove poor in farming terms than that the territory will prove barren in poetic terms.

The poem announces several important features of Kavanagh's approach to writing poetry:

- the use of placenames as a means of staking a poetic claim to the local and the ordinary
- the use of the rhythms and diction of local speech
- the use of humour and self-depreciation.

It also announces an important theme in Kavanagh's work: the poet's eye can see beauty and loveliness in ordinary things. In his focus on the ordinary life of the countryside, Kavanagh sent Irish poetry in a new and exciting direction.

This poem was among Kavanagh's own favourites.

QUESTIONS

1 What is the poet's attitude to 'My black hills' and where is it most in evidence.
2 What are the human qualities that the poet gives to the hills?
3 'My hills hoard the bright shillings of March.' Explore the meaning of this line in the context of the poem and its theme.
4 There is some notable exaggeration in the poem. What is its effect?
5 How is the poverty of the land suggested? Does the poet consider himself poor? Explain your answer.
6 What is the purpose of including the drovers' estimate of the land? Do you think that the poet's heart is really shaken when he hears the drovers?
7 'The sleety winds fondle the rushy beards of Shancoduff.' Comment on the imagery and effect of this line.
8 What, do you think, is the importance of place names in this poem?
9 What features of language are most evident in the poem? What is their effect?
10 Lot's wife is turned to salt for failing to turn her back on the city. What is the relevance of this story to Kavanagh as a man and poet?
11 What is your own response to Patrick Kavanagh, having read this poem?

A CHRISTMAS CHILDHOOD

I
One side of the potato-pits was white with frost—
How wonderful that was, how wonderful!
And when we put our ears to the paling-post
The music that came out was magical.

The light between the ricks of hay and straw   5
Was a hole in Heaven's gable. An apple tree
With its December-glinting fruit we saw—
O you, Eve, were the world that tempted me

To eat the knowledge that grew in clay
And death the germ within it! Now and then   10
I can remember something of the gay
Garden that was childhood's. Again

The tracks of cattle to a drinking-place,
A green stone lying sideways in a ditch
Or any common sight the transfigured face   15
Of a beauty that the world did not touch.

II
My father played the melodion
Outside at our gate;
There were stars in the morning east
And they danced to his music.   20

Across the wild bogs his melodion called
To Lennons and Callans.
As I pulled on my trousers in a hurry
I knew some strange thing had happened.

Outside in the cow-house my mother   25
Made the music of milking;
The light of her stable-lamp was a star
And the frost of Bethlehem made it twinkle.

A water-hen screeched in the bog,
Mass-going feet   30
Crunched the wafer-ice on the pot-holes,
Somebody wistfully twisted the bellows wheel.

My child poet picked out the letters
On the grey stone,
In silver the wonder of a Christmas townland,   35
The winking glitter of a frosty dawn.

Cassiopeia was over
Cassidy's hanging hill,
I looked and three whin bushes rode across
The horizon — the Three Wise Kings.   40

And old man passing said:
'Can't he make it talk'—
The melodion. I hid in the doorway
And tightened the belt of my box-pleated coat.

I nicked six nicks on the door-post   45
With my penknife's big blade—
There was a little one for cutting tobacco.
And I was six Christmases of age.

My father played the melodion,
My mother milked the cows,   50
And I had a prayer like a white rose pinned
On the Virgin Mary's blouse.

GLOSSARY

3 *the paling-post*: a wooden fence post strung with wire

6 *Heaven's gable*: a gable is the triangular part of the end-wall of a house. The child imagines that the light comes from a hole or a window in heaven's gable

8–9 *O you, Eve were the world that tempted me / To eat the knowledge*: in Genesis, God commands Adam and Eve not to eat the fruit of the tree of knowledge, predicting that they will die if they do so. However, the serpent persuades Eve to taste the fruit and she, in turns, gives it to Adam to taste. The knowledge they achieve is the knowledge that they have lost the good of original grace and innocence. As a result of their action, they are banished from Eden. As in 'Advent', Kavanagh renounces knowledge in favour of innocence

15 *transfigured*: changed or glorified. The word takes its resonance in the poem from the Transfiguration of Christ, an incident related in Matthew's gospel, when, in the presence of three apostles, Jesus was transfigured and showed his divine glory

17 *My father played the melodeon*: Kavanagh's father was a well-known musician in the neighbourhood

32 *wistfully*: with sadness or wishfully but with little hope of the wish coming true

37 *Cassiopeia*: a W-shaped constellation in the Northern sky, near the Pole star. For her vanity, Cassiopeia, the mother of Andromeda, was banished to the sky, circling the Pole star forever in her throne, hanging half the time with her head downward

GUIDELINES

Childhood symbolises a lost state of innocent wonder and vision for Kavanagh. Childhood is Kavanagh's Eden. Kavanagh spent some lonely Christmases in Dublin in his flat in Pembroke Road, which served to heighten his remembrance of the Christmases of his childhood. Recalling the period 1947–56, he says, 'I can state that on many Christmas days … I sat in my frowsy flat with nothing to eat and uninvited by anyone'. It is not surprising, then, that in many of the poems written in the early 1940s he remembers his 'childhood country' with affectionate nostalgia. The poverty described in 'The Great Hunger' is overlooked by recreating the past in the voice of a child. In 'A Christmas Childhood', the ordinary farm is transformed by the child's innocent faith. The second part of the poem is wholly successful, the first part is, arguably, less so. Antoinette Quinn suggests that the adult narrator in Part I 'is an obtrusive presence'. However, the first part of the poem establishes the context, the myth of a childhood Eden and the creative force of love, within which the second part of the poem can be understood.

In the second part of 'A Christmas Childhood', there is no adult commentator, and the narrative perspective is that of the child-poet. The garden of childhood is less remembered than reinvented. The poem celebrates the local. Kavanagh lists ordinary farm and household objects and family names. As we read the poem, it is as if the child is offering a running commentary on the events as they unfold at Christmas, so that the past tense of the narrative almost recedes from our consciousness.

The poem succeeds in assimilating the mystery of Christmas into the local setting in a credible way, so that the story of Christmas takes on the vitality of local experience and the local takes on the quality of the divine. Indeed, in the final stanza of the poem the image of the Monaghan family – father, mother and child – have almost become one with the family in Bethlehem.

QUESTIONS

1 The first section of the poem presents us with a series of images from the poet's childhood. Which of them strike you as being most vivid? How different is the Christmas described by Kavanagh to your experience of Christmas, as a child?

2 Explain the reference to knowledge and death in Stanzas 2 and 3.

3 Discuss the meaning of 'the transfigured face / Of a beauty that the world did not touch'.

4 The second section of the poem has a cinematic quality. Outline the series of images that represent the Christmas of the six-year old boy. Which image do you find most appealing?

5 Where, in the second section of the poem, is the divine most evident in the ordinary life of the farm?

6 What vision of family life emerges from the poem? Comment, in particular, on the final stanza of the poem.

7 Examine the language of the poem. Is it 'poetic' or 'conversational', or both?

8 Discuss the view that it is the poet's memory, as a creative force, that is the gateway to an Eden-like world.

9 Are you sympathetic to Kavanagh's desire to return to a childlike innocence? Explain your answer.

10 The two sections were originally published as separate poems. Do you think they work well together? Compare the two sections of the poem in terms of theme and style, including rhyme, imagery and line length.

11 Discuss this poem in the light of 'Advent'.

12 'Kavanagh's achievement is to put a local flavour on a universal mystery.' Do you agree with this assessment of the poem?

13 'In the poem, it is religious faith which is the source of the child's vision of the family farm as a place of wonder.' Give your view of this reading of the poem.

ON RAGLAN ROAD
(Air: 'The Dawning of the Day')

On Raglan Road on an autumn day I met her first and knew
That her dark hair would weave a snare that I might one day rue;
I saw the danger, yet I walked along the enchanted way,
And I said, let grief be a fallen leaf at the dawning of the day.

On Grafton Street in November we tripped lightly along the ledge   5
Of the deep ravine where can be seen the worth of passion's pledge,
The Queen of Hearts still making tarts and I not making hay —
O I loved too much and by such by such is happiness thrown away.

I gave her gifts of the mind I gave her the secret sign that's known
To the artists who have known the true gods of sound and stone   10
And word and tint. I did not stint for I gave her poems to say
With her own name there and her own dark hair like clouds over
    fields of May.

On a quiet street where old ghosts meet I see her walking now
Away from me so hurriedly my reason must allow
That I had wooed not as I should a creature made of clay —   15
When the angel woos the clay he'd lose his wings at the dawn of day.

GLOSSARY

   title *Raglan Road*: Raglan Road in Dublin, close to the Grand Canal, is an area of the
       city in which Kavanagh lived from 1946 to 1959

     2 *a snare*: a trap or a lure; a temptation

     2 *rue*: to regret, usually in relation to something that has bitter consequences

     5 *Grafton Street*: then, as now, the most fashionable street in the city.

  10–11 *the artists…of sound and stone / And word and tint*: musicians, sculptors, writers
       and painters

    15 *a creature made of clay*: in the enchantment of love the lover saw his beloved as
       a heavenly creature, an angel. Now he realises that she is mortal, made of clay,
       and, therefore, imperfect

GUIDELINES

The poem was first published in 1946 under the title, 'Dark Haired Miriam Ran Away'. Miriam was the name of his brother's girlfriend. In fact, the poem charts Kavanagh's infatuation with Hilda Moriarty, a young medical student, who later married Donough O'Malley, a minister in the Fianna Fáil governments of the 1960s. In the poems which deal with love, Kavanagh often presents himself as attractive to women, by virtue of being a poet, yet unsuccessful in love.

The ballad tells the story of unrequited love. The events are viewed through the disappointment of hindsight. Like many ballads, 'On Raglan Road' cautions against loving too much and placing one's trust in the promises of new love.

The poem was written during a period when much of Kavanagh's poetry expresses an angry disappointment with his life and career as a poet, and reveals his anxieties and insecurities. 'On Raglan Road' is gentler than most of his writing of this time, though it is still concerned with the theme of failure. The poem carries a succession of feelings – sorrow, regret, pride and arrogance – all centred on the poet. (The word 'I' appears fourteen times!)

The poem is set to the music of the traditional air, 'The Dawning of the Day'. Luke Kelly's recording of the song is considered the definitive version.

QUESTIONS

1 The poem tells a story of unrequited love. Where is the evidence that the feeling was all on one side? What is the predominant tone of the poem?

2 What attitude is suggested by the words 'let grief be a fallen leaf'?

3 Comment on the sentiments expressed by the speaker in the second stanza. Do they show him in a favourable light?

4 What are the gifts that the poet gives to his beloved, as described in Stanza 3?

5 In the final stanza the beloved is now seen as 'a creature made of clay'. Comment on this. Does the poem succeed in giving us a view of the real woman?

6 Discuss the meaning of the final line of the poem. Is there a suggestion that love robs the poet of his inspiration?

7 Here are three views of the poet's presentation of himself in the poem:
   - the poet presents himself as an angel who has wooed an unworthy creature. To the reader, the young woman has had a lucky escape
   - the self-presentation in the poem is characterised by humour and irony
   - Kavanagh presents himself as a child confused and hurt by love.
   Discuss these views of the poet's presentation of himself in the poem.

8 'There is something both ridiculous and heartbreaking in "Raglan Road"'. Do you think this is a fair assessment of the poem?

DENISE LEVERTOV

1923–1997

BIOGRAPHY

Denise Levertov was born in Essex in England. Her father, raised as a Jew, converted to Christianity while attending university in Germany. By the time of Denise's birth, he was an Anglican parson, settled in England. Her mother was Welsh and traced her ancestry back to a Welsh mystic. Not surprisingly, given her family background, Levertov's poetry often has a spiritual, mystical quality, that celebrates the sacredness of all living things.

Denise Levertov was educated at home and was writing poetry from an early age. During the Second World War, she worked as a nurse in London. Her first book of poetry was published immediately after the war, to wide acclaim. In 1947 Denise Levertov married the American writer, Mitchell Goodman, and moved to the United States, becoming a naturalised citizen in 1956. Her poems, published throughout the 1950s and 1960s, brought recognition from critics and writers alike, including William Carlos Williams, with whom she corresponded.

During the 1960s, the Vietnam War and feminism became central concerns in her work. Her 1967 collection *The Sorrow Dance* is among her finest books.

Up to the time of her death in 1997, Denise Levertov continued to write and publish poetry, translations and essays.

1) Did the people of Vietnam
   use lanterns of stone?
2) Did they hold ceremonies
   to reverence the opening of buds?
3) Were they inclined to rippling laughter?   5
4) Did they use bone and ivory,
   jade and silver, for ornament?
5) Had they an epic poem?
6) Did they distinguish between speech and singing?

1) Sir, their light hearts turned to stone.   10
   It is not remembered whether in gardens
   stone lanterns illumined pleasant ways.
2) Perhaps they gathered once to delight in blossom,
   but after the children were killed
   there were no more buds.   15
3) Sir, laughter is bitter to the burned mouth.
4) A dream ago, perhaps. Ornament is for joy.
   All the bones were charred.
5) It is not remembered. Remember,
   most were peasants; their life   20
   was in rice and bamboo.
   When peaceful clouds were reflected in the paddies
   and the water-buffalo stepped surely along terraces,
   maybe fathers told their sons old tales.
   When bombs smashed the mirrors   25
   there was time only to scream.
6) There is an echo yet, it is said,
   of their speech which was like a song.
   It is reported their singing resembled
   the flight of moths in moonlight.   30
   Who can say? It is silent now.

GLOSSARY

title *What Were They Like:* the 'They' of the title are the people of Vietnam. The poem contrasts the people before and after the Vietnam War. From the nineteenth century until 1954, Vietnam was a colony of France. When the French withdrew, the country was divided in two, with a communist government in the north, supported by China and Russia, and a government in the south, supported by America. By 1959, North and South Vietnam were at war. In 1962 American troops took part in their first combat mission against Vietcong (North Vietnamese) forces. As their involvement in the war increased, American forces sprayed large areas of land with chemicals and fire-bombed villages where Vietcong forces were thought to be hiding. Despite a massive number of American troops (500,000 at the height of the war in the mid-1960s) the North overcame the South and the country was reunited in 1976. The last American combat troops withdrew from Vietnam in 1973. In all, three million American soldiers served in Vietnam, while 58,000 were killed. Over a million Vietnamese soldiers, from both sides, died in the war and hundreds of thousands of civilians were killed

7 *jade:* an ornamental stone of varying shades of green

8 *an epic poem:* a long poem, often telling the mythical history of a people or nation

22 *paddies:* water-filled fields where rice is grown

GUIDELINES

Levertov is sometimes described as a poet of memory and commemoration, with a religious-like sense of the sacredness of life. These qualities are evident in 'What Were They Like?', which remembers the ordered life of the Vietnamese before the war and laments the deaths of Vietnamese children in the American bombing campaign.

The poem is structured through a series of questions and answers. The questions succeed in calling to mind images of a sophisticated culture, and a gentle and artistic people. The answers indicate how the war has changed everything for the people of Vietnam.

The answer to question five gives a picture of the traditional life of the Vietnamese peasant: the paddies, the water-buffalo, the sky reflected in the water of the fields and fathers and sons working side-by-side. The image has a timeless and peaceful quality about it. The image of the bomb destroying the peace of the fields reveals Levertov's view of war as destructive and irrational. War makes us lose sight of what is real and important. War blurs our vision. War causes us to forget what it is we value.

The final answer ends with the grim conclusion, 'It is silent now'. Before the silence it was reported that the singing of the people resembled 'the flights of moths in moonlight'. The image suggests something light, delicate and graceful. The silence that closes the poem is haunted by the echo of an earlier time.

Whose are the voices in the poem? Is the first voice the voice of a reasonable, civilised American? Is it the voice of an American with no more than a vague interest in Vietnam? Or is it the voice of a repentant American? Might the speaker be a current or former member of the American army, who served in Vietnam? Is it the voice of the victimiser?

Is the second voice the voice of an anguished Vietnamese? Is it the voice of a second-generation Vietnamese? Is it the voice of someone who has survived the war? Is it the voice of a victim?

You might find it an interesting exercise to imagine a scenario in which these questions and answers are asked and answered. Decide on a location and the circumstances in which this would take place.

'What Were They Like?' is an anti-war poem. The poem concentrates on what has been lost and destroyed – children, and the culture and customs of a gentle and civilised people. Many of the phrases offer a summary of the outcome of the war: 'hearts turned to stone', 'the children were killed', 'bones were charred', 'bombs smashed' and 'there was only time to scream'. These outcomes relate to any war, not just the war in Vietnam. The tone of the poem is quietly angry and sad. Despite its unusual question and answer structure, the poem has many 'poetic' features. Note the use of repetition both in the structure of sentences and in sounds. Levertov uses words with long vowel sounds to create a formal effect which, in the final two answers, turns to elegy.

QUESTIONS

1 Who, do you think, is the 'Sir' of the poem?

2 a) Comment on the tone in which 'Sir' puts his questions.
   b) What words capture this tone?
   c) The questions are in the past tense. What is the significance of this?
   d) What kind of world and people are suggested by these questions?
   e) Do the questions suggest that the questioner has some knowledge of Vietnam and its culture?

3 Who, do you think, provides the answers to the questions? Support your answer by quotation from the poem.

4 'It is not remembered'. From the answers to the questions, describe Vietnam before the war and describe it since the war.

5 Look at the answers numbered 2–4. Which of the short concise statements strike you as having most effect. Give reasons for your answer.

JOHN MONTAGUE

B. 1929

BIOGRAPHY

John Montague was born in Brooklyn, New York, on 28 February, 1929. His parents were Irish emigrants. During the war of Independence, his father James was an Irish volunteer whose activities included participation in ambushes and house-burning. He emigrated to New York in 1925. In Ireland, he had been unsuccessful in business ventures financed from the sale of his farm. He became a ticket collector in the New York subway. His wife and two young sons joined him later.

John left New York at the age of four with his mother and two brothers when his father could no longer support the family. Although his mother also returned to Tyrone, she took little or no part in his upbringing. He was reared by two aunts who lived in his father's home in Garvaghey and he grew up without knowing his father.

He was educated at Garvaghey Primary School and later at St Patrick's College Armagh. In 1946, he won a scholarship to University College Dublin. He later studied at Yale and Berkeley, two famous American Universities. One of his teachers at St Patrick's College was Sean O'Boyle, a leading authority on Ulster folksong and Irish poetry. O'Boyle gave him a love of the Gaelic tradition, which was to have a profound influence on his life and on his poetry.

Montague published his first collection of poems, *Forms of Exile*, in 1958. In the 1960s, he taught Anglo-Irish literature at UCD and in 1967 he issued *A Chosen Light*. In the late 1960s he responded with enthusiasm to the Northern Ireland Civil Rights Movement and dedicated a collection of poems, *A New Siege*, to Bernadette Devlin, our of the leaders of the movement.

In 1972, he published *The Rough Field*, in which he explored Ulster and family history. Other important collections of his poetry include *A Slow Dance* (1975); *Poisoned Lands* (1977); *The Great Cloak* (1975); *Selected Poems* (1982) and *The Dead Kingdom* (1984). *A Slow Dance* is particularly interesting for its treatment of the Northern Ireland conflict. In one of the poems in that collection, 'Falls Funeral', there is a chillingly realistic account of the burial of a murdered Catholic child. In another, 'Northern Express', Montague shows how the horrors of the struggle can affect ordinary people. Some of the poems in *The Dead Kingdom* deal with his father's lonely life in Brooklyn.

Montague has held a wide variety of positions throughout his adult life. He has been a film-critic, a proof-reader, an editor, a university lecturer and a writer-in-residence at many American universities. In 1998 he was appointed to The Ireland Chair of Poetry, which is supported by the Ireland Fund. Since the 1970s, he has been based in Cork, lecturing at University College there and running poetry workshops. He was the first significant twentieth-century poet writing from a Northern Irish Catholic background. He established a tradition which has been followed by others from a similar background, including Seamus Heaney.

THE LOCKET

Sing a last song
for the lady who has gone,
fertile source of guilt and pain.
The worst birth in the annals of Brooklyn,
that was my cue to come on,   5
my first claim to fame.

Naturally, she longed for a girl,
and all my infant curls of brown
couldn't excuse my double blunder
coming out, both the wrong sex,   10
and the wrong way around.
Not readily forgiven,

So you never nursed me
and when all my father's songs
couldn't sweeten the lack of money,   15
when poverty comes through the door
love flies up the chimney,
your favourite saying.

Then you gave me away,
might never have known me,   20
if I had not cycled down
to court you like a young man,
teasingly untying your apron,
drinking by the fire, yarning

Of your wild, young days   25
which didn't last long, for you,
lovely Molly, the belle of your small town,
landed up mournful and chill
as the constant rain that lashes it,
wound into your cocoon of pain.   30

Standing in that same hallway,
don't come again, you say, roughly,
I start to get fond of you, John,
and then you are up and gone;
the harsh logic of a forlorn woman   35
resigned to being alone.

And still, mysterious blessing,
I never knew, until you were gone,
that, always around your neck,
you wore an oval locket
with an old picture in it,   40
of a child in Brooklyn.

GLOSSARY

2 *the lady*: this is the poet's mother

3 *fertile source of guilt and pain*: the poet's mother inspired strong feelings of guilt and pain in him

4 *Brooklyn*: Montague was born in Brooklyn, New York

5–6 *that was … fame*: his troublesome birth was the first remarkable thing about him

12 *Not readily forgiven*: his mother did not easily forgive him for being a boy and for having caused her such pain at his birth

13 *you never nursed me*: you treated me coldly.

14–15 *and when … money*: his father did not have a well-paid job and also drank too much. His songs could not compensate for the poverty his mother was forced to live in

19 *Then you gave me away*: when he returned to Ireland at the age of 4, he was raised, not by his mother, but by two aunts

24 *yarning*: telling stories

27 *lovely Molly*: a reference to the Rose of Mooncoin, a famous Irish ballad

27 *belle*: beautiful girl

28 *landed up*: ended up

29–30 *as the constant … cocoon of pain*: her efforts to protect herself from grief were not successful

30 *cocoon*: a protective covering. In this case it means a retreat from the sorrows of life

35 *forlorn*: pitifully sad and lonely

38 *gone*: dead

GUIDELINES

This is one of a number of poems in which Montague deals with members of his family. For example, in 'The Cage' he writes about his father. His mother is the main subject of 'The Locket'; another is the unusual relationship between mother and son. The background of the poem is a sad one. His mother, having given birth to two boys, resented John's birth because she wanted a girl: he thus felt, and was made to feel, that he should carry a burden of guilt for having been born, more particularly as his birth was a difficult one for his mother. Following the return of both of them to Ireland, his mother refused to let him live with her; he was obliged to live with his parental aunts seven miles away and endure the emotional consequences of his parents' broken marriage.

The poem is a lament for the poet's dead mother. It is not a conventional lament for a dead person: the poet is much more interested in the influence of his mother on his life than in her significance as a woman. Through most of the poem, the emphasis is on the damaging influence of his mother on his own life and development. She did not welcome his birth and found it hard to forgive him for it. She never nurtured him, and gave him away rather than rear him. She discouraged his visits in order to avoid growing fond of him. In this she follows 'the harsh logic of a forlorn woman / resigned to being alone'.

Rejection is not, however, the entire story of the poem, which ends with the poet's experience of what he calls a 'mysterious blessing'. After her death, it transpires that his mother always wore an oval locket containing an old picture of the poet as a child.

In 'The Locket', as in many of Montague's poems, among them 'Like Dolmens Round my Childhood, The Old People' and 'The Wild Dog Rose', outward appearances can be profoundly deceptive.

On a first reading the fourth stanza of the poem may seem odd. The poet claims that his mother might never have known him if he had not cycled the seven miles separating his home from hers. The purpose of his visit was:

> to court you like a young man
> teasingly untying your apron,
> drinking by the fire, yarning …

These ritual visits are best explained by the idea that the young Montague is not making them merely in an attempt to heal the wound of being an unwanted child. There is a sense in which he sees himself as his father's double as he does in 'The Cage', and even more obviously in a poem called 'The Same Fault', where he remarks that he and his father have:

the same scar

in the same place

as if the same fault ran through us both.

The child's mental anguish at being a displaced, unwanted child is mirrored in his father's anguish at losing his family, since, as a husband, he is unwanted. His wife, having instinctively rejected their child, engages in a double rejection when she refuses to live in New York as an immigrant wife and leaves her husband to return to Ireland. The boy's understanding of his father's predicament may well help to explain why he is willing to assume the role of his father's double, wooing his mother as if on his own father's behalf and vainly trying to heal the wounds of family division.

QUESTIONS

1 The title of the poem and the last stanza emphasise the importance of the locket. Why is the locket so important to the poet?

2 How would you describe the tone of the first stanza?

3 When the poet describes his coming into the world as 'The worst birth in the annals of Brooklyn' (line 4), are we to take him seriously? Explain your answer.

4 Montague describes his mother as a 'fertile source of guilt and pain' (line 3). How is this description illustrated in the rest of the poem?

5 Show how the poet explores the theme of rejection throughout the poem.

6 The poem gives us an idea of the poet's attitude to his mother. How would you describe this attitude?

7 What does the poem tell us about the mother's life?

8 How does the young Montague try to win his mother's affection? Does he succeed?

9 Write an account of the young Montague's relationship with his mother, based on this poem.

10 What has happened to make the mother of the poet 'a forlorn woman'? You might look particularly at Stanza 3.

11 Is the poet sorry for himself? Give reasons for your answer.

12 What is the happiest moment of the poem, and what is the saddest?

THE CAGE

My father, the least happy
man I have known. His face
retained the pallor
of those who work underground:
the lost years in Brooklyn   5
listening to a subway
shudder the earth.

But a traditional Irishman
who (released from his grille
in the Clark St I.R.T.)   10
drank neat whiskey until
he reached the only element
he felt at home in
any longer: brute oblivion.

And yet picked himself   15
up, most mornings,
to march down the street
extending his smile
to all sides of the good
(non-negro) neighbourhood   20
belled by St. Teresa's church.

When he came back
we walked together
across fields of Garvaghey
to see hawthorn on the summer   25
hedges, as though
he had never left;
a bend on the road

which still sheltered
primroses. But we
did not smile in
the shared complicity
of a dream, for when
weary Odysseus returns
Telemachus must leave.

Often as I descend
into subway or underground
I see his bald head behind
the bars of the small booth;
the mark of an old car
accident beating on his
ghostly forehead.

30

35

40

GLOSSARY

3 *pallor*: an unnatural paleness

5 *Brooklyn*: a borough of New York. Many Irish emigrants lived there

6 *subway*: New York underground rail system

7 *shudder*: to shake violently

9 *grille*: a metal screen with bars. His duties as a subway ticket collector meant that the poet's father had to work behind a grille. Here it refers to the subway ticket office where the poet's father worked

10 *the Clark St I.R.T.*: a New York subway station

11 *neat whiskey*: undiluted whiskey

12 *the only element*: the only condition

14 *oblivion*: forgetfulness

18 *extending*: reaching out with

19–21 *to all sides … … church*: the speaker's father was happy to smile at the white inhabitants of the white neighbourhood, served by the local Catholic Church

22 *came back*: returned to Ireland

24 *Garvaghey*: the birthplace of the poet's father, who returned to Ireland in 1952, nineteen years after John had been sent back

29–32 *But we …of a dream*: we did not share the same dreams, hopes or ambitions

31 *complicity*: involvement

32–34 *for when … must leave*: Odysseus, also called Ulysses, is the hero of Homer's Epic poem, *The Odyssey*. His adventures on land and on sea last twenty years. Telemachus is the son of Odysseus. In Homer's poem, Telemachus and his mother Penelope wait at their home in Ithaca for the return of Odysseus. When Odysseus comes home, Telemachus leaves Ithaca. There are obvious parallels between this story and that of the Montague family. The most striking one is that the younger Montague left for New York as soon as his father came back from there

39 *booth*: a small enclosed structure

GUIDELINES

The poem is about Montague's father, James. It is also about the father-son relationship, and about the effects of exile and return on a man described in Stanza 2 as 'a traditional Irishman'. Montague's father, 'the least happy / man I have known', according to the poet, had every reason to be unhappy. His militant patriotism induced him to flee to New York. His failure to earn an adequate living and his fondness for drink alienated his wife for whom, as we learn in 'The Locket', all his songs 'couldn't sweeten the lack of money'.

Abandoned by his wife and family in the early 1930s, he was obliged to live alone in New York until his retirement from a menial job in 1952, when he returned to Ireland to live out the last seven years of his life in Omagh, Co Tyrone.

The first three stanzas of the poem provide a concise account of James Montague's life as an Irish emigrant in New York. It is significant that Montague describes his father's time in New York as 'the lost years'. The suggestion here is that exile from the place of his ancestors deprives his life of its essential meaning and robs him of his identity. The title of the poem is a metaphor for James Montague's plight. He spends his working life underground in a subway ticket office, a kind of miniature prison in which he must dispense tickets through the bars of a grille. He is pale-faced from lack of fresh air, his ears assaulted by the noise of the subway trains as they 'shudder the earth'. His pale colour suggests death, which is also brought to mind by the image of the underground. This word invokes thoughts of Hades, the home of the dead in Greek mythology. Compare the parallel imagery in 'All Legendary Obstacles'.

What he has lost through exile is suggested in Stanzas 4 and 5: the fields of his native Garvaghey, 'hawthorn on the summer / hedges' and primroses sheltered by a bend in the road. Life in the infernal underground cage can be relieved only in the 'brute oblivion' of drunkenness, another kind of imprisonment. The contrast between these forms of physical and mental captivity and the freedom of the open fields of Garvaghey is central to the meaning of the poem. James Montague's underground life behind the grille of the Clark Street subway station becomes a metaphor for his life as an exile who cannot feel at home in New York and who tries to find a substitute home in a state of forgetfulness induced by neat whiskey. The cage suggests another kind of double life. He is visible through its bars and at the same time cut off from a world to which he does not fully belong.

Stanzas 4 and 5 refer to James Montague's return from America in 1952, when father and son could spend time together in Garvaghey. The end of the father's exile does not, however, mark the beginning of a happy relationship between father and son. They 'did not smile in / the shared complicity / of a dream'. When James Montague, like the weary Odysseus of Homer's ancient epic, comes home, his son, like Telemachus, son of Odysseus, must himself go into exile. His place of exile is New York, the one originally chosen by his father.

The final stanza of the poem is based on the notion that the father is a double for his son, just as the son is a double for him. To reinforce this point, Montague uses an image of his dead father behind the bars of a subway booth:

> *the mark of an old car*
> *accident beating on his*
> *ghostly forehead.*

Elsewhere in his work, Montague is at pains to stress the physical resemblance between his father and himself, in particular the detail of a facial scar common to both as a means of suggesting that he sees his father as an image of himself. (See the reference to 'The Same Fault' in the commentary on 'The Locket'.)

QUESTIONS

1 Why do you think the poet chose 'The Cage' as the title of this poem? Explore the ideas associated with the image of the cage throughout the poem.

2 How would you describe the poet's attitude to his father? Refer to words or phrases in the poem.

3 Explain the reference to 'the lost years in Brooklyn'.

4 Why did the poet's father seek comfort in 'brute oblivion'?

5 The poet tells us that his father extended his smile 'to all sides of the good / (non-negro) neighbourhood'. Explain this reference.

6 How is the idea of imprisonment suggested in Stanza 2 of the poem?

7 In Stanza 5, we are told that father and son did not smile in 'the shared complicity / of a dream'. Why do you think this was so? What was the dream?

8 Comment on the reference to Odysseus and Telemachus in Stanza 5.

9 Say what you like or dislike about this poem.

10 On the evidence of the poem, does the father's life seem to have served any purpose?

11 The poem features some significant examples of contrast. Discuss some of these, for example, the contrast between Brooklyn and Garvaghey.

12 What do the images in the final stanza of the poem suggest to you ('I descend'; 'underground'; 'bars'; 'ghostly forehead')?

LIKE DOLMENS ROUND MY CHILDHOOD, THE OLD PEOPLE

Like dolmens round my childhood, the old people.

Jamie MacCrystal sang to himself,
A broken song without tune, without words;
He tipped me a penny every pension day,
Fed kindly crusts to winter birds   5
When he died, his cottage was robbed,
Mattress and money box torn and searched.
Only the corpse they didn't disturb.

Maggie Owens was surrounded by animals,
A mongrel bitch and shivering pups,   10
Even in her bedroom a she-goat cried.
She was a well of gossip defiled,
Fanged chronicler of a whole countryside:
Reputed a witch, all I could find
Was her lonely need to deride.   15

The Nialls lived along a mountain lane
Where heather bells bloomed, clumps of foxglove.
All were blind, with Blind Pension and Wireless,
Dead eyes serpent-flicked as one entered
To shelter from a downpour of mountain rain.
Crickets chirped under the rocking hearthstone   20
Until the muddy sun shone out again.

Mary Moore lived in a crumbling gatehouse,
Famous as Pisa for its leaning gable.
Bag-apron and boots, she tramped the fields
Driving lean cattle from a miry stable.   25
A by-word for fierceness, she fell asleep
Over love stories, Red Star and Red Circle,
Dreamed of gypsy love rites, by firelight sealed.

Wile Billy Eagleson married a Catholic servant girl   30
When all his Loyal family passed on:
We danced round him shouting 'To Hell with King Billy,'
And dodged from the arc of his flailing blackthorn.
Forsaken by both creeds, he showed little concern
Until the Orange drums banged past in the summer   35
And bowler and sash aggressively shone.

Curate and doctor trudged to attend them,
Through knee-deep snow, through summer heat,
From main road to lane to broken path,
Gulping the mountain air with painful breath.   40
Sometimes they were found by neighbours,
Silent keepers of a smokeless hearth,
Suddenly cast in the mould of death.

Ancient Ireland, indeed! I was reared by her bedside,
The rune and the chant, evil eye and averted head,   45
Fomorian fierceness of family and local feud.
Gaunt figures of fear and of friendliness,
For years they trespassed on my dreams,
Until once, in a standing circle of stones,
I felt their shadows pass   50

Into that dark permanence of ancient forms.

GLOSSARY

1 *dolmens*: prehistoric monuments usually consisting of several great stone slabs set edgewise in the earth to support a flat stone, which served as a roof. Dolmens were designed as burial structures

12 *She was ...defiled*: she told foul stories about her neighbours

13 *Fanged chronicler*: teller of bitter, biting stories

14 *Reputed a witch*: having the reputation of being a witch

15 *Was her lonely need to deride*: her loneliness caused her to mock other people

18 *All were blind ... Wireless*: those who were blind were entitled to a pension and a radio from the social welfare services

23 *gatehouse*: a house occupied by the caretaker of a larger house

24 *Pisa*: a reference to the leaning tower in that city

25 *miry*: muddy

27 *Red Star and Red Circle*: magazines featuring love stories

31 *Loyal family*: a family which supported the connection between Northern Ireland and the United Kingdom

32 *King Billy*: King William of Orange, a Protestant hero

34 *Forsaken by both creeds*: abandoned by members of both religions

35 *Until the Orange drums ... summer*: until the arrival of the Orange Order marching season

36 *bowler and sash*: these are worn by members of the Orange Order during their marches

37 *Curate*: Catholic priest

45 *rune and chant*: a rune was a song or set of words believed to have magic properties. The chant has a similar meaning

46 *evil eye and averted head*: people who had the evil eye were believed to have the power to bring disaster on those they looked at. To avoid this, people turned away or averted their heads

47 *Fomorian*: the Fomorians were a savage tribe of ancient settlers in Ireland

47 *feud*: long-standing dispute often involving several generations of the same families

47 *Gaunt*: thin

48 *trespassed on my dreams*: invaded my dreams

49 *standing circle of stones*: in ancient Ireland, stone circles were associated with the worship of the sun

50–51 *I felt their shadows pass ... forms*: the ancient forms that haunted him have passed away forever

GUIDELINES

This poem deals with some of the more unusual people who inhabited the world of Montague's childhood. Like many of Montague's poems, this one features fully human individuals, scarred by misery and suffering but also possessing faith and enjoying life. The main characters in the poem are isolated, lonely people. For the young Montague, their main significance was that they haunted his childhood dreams, conjuring up sinister and grotesque images associated with ancient pagan customs. In early adult life, when childhood gave way to manhood, the dark dreams no longer troubled him. He traces his liberation from their fearful grip to a single experience. Standing as a young man in a circle of stones, he feels the terrible shadow cast by the old people pass away and the dreams, which have troubled him are transformed into myth, 'that dark permanence of ancient forms'.

The dolmens mentioned in the title and in the first line of the poem have a symbolic meaning. By imagining the old people as dolmens, the poet is suggesting why Jamie Mac Crystal, Maggie Owens and the others dominated his life and troubled even his dreams. He was imprisoned by their influence in much the same way as the body of an ancient inhabitant of Ireland was buried beneath a dolmen. There is a further dimension to the comparison between dolmens and old people. To the poet's eye, the human figures are scattered around the landscape like figures of stone.

The poem, however, is one of liberation as well as of imprisonment. This becomes clear in the last stanza. Just as the dolmens represent the child's captivity, the standing circle of stones is associated with his release from the fearful dreams inspired by the old people. The last stanza tells us that his escape from the shadow cast on his young life by his elderly neighbours coincides with his entry into manhood. The act of making the old people present in his poetry serves a purpose similar to exorcism. They become in the end external to his mind and find their permanence in stone.

To the child's imagination all the characters of the poem are forbidding, abnormal and sometimes grotesque. Jamie Mac Crystal's song without tune and without words is sung to himself. Maggie Owens is thought to be a witch and keeps a she-goat in her bedroom. The Nialls are all blind. Mary Moore is remarkable for her fierceness, while Billy Eagleson is wild and wields a flailing blackthorn. These primitive people carry on some of the pagan traditions of ancient Ireland. There is, however, more to them than this. They may be 'Gaunt figures of fear', but as the last stanza admits they also appeal to the poet's imagination as figures of friendliness. In spite of their forbidding appearance the poet is able to feel sympathy for them and to understand the motives behind their behaviour. Jamie Mac Crystal is a poor man but still gives a penny to the young Montague every pension day and feeds hungry winter birds. Maggie Owens is a notorious gossip but the poet feels able to explain this by suggesting that frustration and loneliness cause her to speak ill of her neighbours. We find a similar attitude in 'The Wild Dog Rose' where the woman described as a hag is really an ordinary human being who has suffered much in her isolation.

QUESTIONS

1 In the title and in the first line, the poet relates the old people to dolmens. What is the significance of this relationship?

2 The old people mentioned in the poem have a few things in common. Mention as many of these as you can.

3 What is the poet's attitude to the people he is describing. Explain your answer by referring to words or phrases from the poem.

4 Which of the people do you think had a) the happiest life, and b) the saddest life. Refer to the poem for examples.

5 Maggie Owens is not the woman she seems. Explain this idea.

6 The old people are described as 'Silent keepers of a smokeless hearth / Suddenly cast in the mould of death'. What does this mean? Has 'mould' more than one meaning in this context?

7 Is the poem sad or comic or both? Explain.

8 Choose your favourite character from the poem. Give reasons for your choice.

9 Why is Billy Eagleson 'forsaken by both creeds'? What effect do the 'Orange drums' have on his attitudes?

10 What does the poet mean when he claims that he was reared by the bedside of 'Ancient Ireland'? Develop your answer by referring to the poem.

11 Why do you think the poet describes his neighbours as 'Gaunt figures of fear and friendliness'?

12 How did the old people trespass on the poet's dreams? How did he free himself from the influence of these dreams?

EDWIN MORGAN

B. 1920

BIOGRAPHY

Edward Morgan was born in Glasgow in 1920. He was attending university when the Second World War broke out. He left his studies and joined the Royal Army Medical Corps. He completed his degree in 1947 and then worked in the English Department of Glasgow University until his retirement in 1980.

In the late 1950s, Morgan looked to American and Russian writers for inspiration. He drew on the example of William Carlos Williams for a kind of poetry that related to ordinary life using direct and everyday language. In the 1960s Morgan made contact with a number of Brazilian poets, whose work he admired for its use of ordinary language, humour and its political concerns.

Since the publication of his first collection in 1949, Edwin Morgan has published sixteen books of poetry. His poetry covers a wide range of styles and subject matter, from epic sea poems to his more recent science fiction narratives. He is one of the great innovators and jokers of poetry, playing with language, ideas and the latest forms of information technology. Like many contemporary poets, Morgan is also at home in more traditional forms. His Glasgow sonnets are an impressive set of poems about his native city. He uses the dialect of the city for many of his poems.

Morgan has also written for the stage and translated poetry from twelve languages. 'Strawberries' is one of a number of intense, personal love poems that he has written, noted for their directness and honesty.

STRAWBERRIES

There were never strawberries
like the ones we had
that sultry afternoon
sitting on the step
of the open french window   5
facing each other
your knees held in mine
the blue plates in our laps
the strawberries glistening
in the hot sunlight   10
we dipped them in sugar
looking at each other
not hurrying the feast
for one to come
the empty plates   15
laid on the stone together
with the two forks crossed
and I bent towards you
sweet in that air
in my arms   20
abandoned like a child
from your eager mouth
the taste of strawberries
in my memory
lean back again let me love you   25

let the sun beat
on our forgetfulness
one hour of all
the heat intense
and summer lightening   30
on the Kilpatrick hills

let the storm wash the plates

GLOSSARY

title *Strawberries*: the red of the strawberries and the sweet taste of their soft flesh make the fruit an apt symbol for the pleasures of sensual love

3 *sultry*: hot and humid. The word also has the meaning of 'full of pleasure'

8 *the blue plates in our laps*: note the number of 'p', 'b', 't' and 's' sounds in the poem, which imitate the savouring of food, and suggest the savouring of kisses

17 *the two forks crossed*: the crossed forks form an x, a symbol of love. They also suggest that the feast is not over. Is there, perhaps, a hint that the love described in the poem is same-sex love?

31 *Kilpatrick Hills*: a range of hills west of Glasgow

GUIDELINES

In this love poem, the speaker remembers an afternoon with his/her beloved and looks to a renewal of their love.

The first seventeen lines of the long first stanza set the scene of 'that sultry afternoon'. The day was warm and sunny, the strawberries glistened in the 'hot sunlight'. There is a sense of leisure, of unhurried enjoyment. The lovers remain seated after the plates and the glasses have been emptied, lingering in the moment, anticipating the feast of passionate love that is to follow.

At the end of the first stanza and continuing into the second, the poem moves into the present as the speaker urges a renewal of their love. The speaker plays on the idea of memory and forgetfulness. The memory of love may lead them to forget everything else and abandon themselves, again, in love.

The image of the summer lightening can be read as a symbol of the lovers passion – warm and electrifying – though it can also be read in a darker light, suggesting that the love may be subject to destructive forces.

Does the final line, 'let the storm wash the plates' suggest that the 'you' does not have the same interest in renewing the love? Does it suggest that their passion has been washed away by time?

The absence of punctuation in the poem and the lack of conventions and rules reinforces the idea of passion, of a kind of love that cares little for rules and regulations. The absence of punctuation also contributes to the blurring of the distinction between the past and the present.

Whether or not the lovers renew their love, the poem succeeds in recreating and celebrating a remembered moment of love and conveys that moment in vivid, immediate terms. The senses of taste, touch and sight are invoked. Even the placing of the plates side-by-side, and the crossing of the forks, has a romantic resonance. This suggests that one of the themes of the poem is the way in which everything, including otherwise trivial details, are transformed in the eye of love.

QUESTIONS

1 Comment on the title of the poem. Do you think it is an appropriate one?
2 What details, do you think, are most vivid in this poem?
3 Examine how Edwin Morgan uses long vowels, soft sounds, rhymes and echoes to create a sensuous mood.
4 What do you think of the lack of punctuation in the poem? Does it add or take from your enjoyment? Indicate where you would place the most important pauses in the poem.
5 What, in your view, is the significance of the 'two forks crossed'?
6 '… let the storm wash the plates'. Is this a good ending to the poem? Explain your answer.
7 Why, do you think, does the speaker recall the afternoon of the strawberries? In your view, are the lovers still as united as they were on that day? What line in the poem, in your view, tells you most about the relationship between the lovers?
8 Do you think the poem works as a love poem? Explain your answer.
9 Select your two favourite lines or phrases from the poem and say why you chose them.
10 Select a piece of music that you think would make a good accompaniment to 'Strawberries' and explain your choice.

PAUL MULDOON

B. 1951

BIOGRAPHY

Paul Muldoon was born in Portadown, Co. Armagh on 20 June, 1951. His mother was a teacher, his father a labourer and market gardener. He was educated at St Patrick's College, Armagh, and at the Queen's University, Belfast, where the poet Seamus Heaney was his tutor. Muldoon's first collection of poems, *New Weather*, was published in 1973 while he was 22 and still at university.

Muldoon has worked as a radio and television producer for BBC Northern Ireland and he has held writing fellowships at various universities including Cambridge University, Columbia University (New York) and the University of California at Berkeley. Since 1990 he has been a Professor of the Humanities and Creative Writing at Princeton University.

Muldoon has received many awards for his poetry, including the Sir Geoffrey Faber Memorial Award in 1991, the T. S. Eliot Memorial Prize in 1994 for his collection *The Annals of Chile* and the American Academy of Arts and Letters Award for Literature in 1996. In May 1999 he was appointed Professor of Poetry at Oxford University. His *New Selected Poems 1968–1994*, published in 1996, won the prestigious *Irish Times* Irish Literature Prize for Poetry in 1997. He has edited a number of poetry anthologies, among them *The Faber Book of Contemporary Irish Poetry* (1986), and he has also written a play for television, *Monkeys* (1989). His collection *Moy Sand and Gravel* (2002) was awarded the Pulitzer Prize in 2003.

He lives in the USA with his novelist wife Jean Hanff Korelitz and their daughter.

ANSEO

When the Master was calling the roll
At the primary school in Collegelands,
You were meant to call back *Anseo*
And raise your hand
As your name occurred.   5
Anseo, meaning here, here and now,
All present and correct,
Was the first word of Irish I spoke.
The last name on the ledger
Belonged to Joseph Mary Plunkett Ward   10
And was followed, as often as not,
By silence, knowing looks,
A nod and a wink, the Master's droll
'And where's our little Ward-of-court?'

I remember the first time he came back   15
The Master had sent him out
Along the hedges
To weigh up for himself and cut
A stick with which he would be beaten.
After a while, nothing was spoken;   20
He would arrive as a matter of course
With an ash-plant, a salley-rod.
Or finally, the hazel-wand
He had whittled down to a whip-lash,
Its twist of red and yellow lacquers   25
Sanded and polished,
And altogether so delicately wrought
That he had engraved his initials on it.

I last met Joseph Mary Plunkett Ward
In a pub just over the Irish border. 30
He was living in the open,
In a secret camp
On the other side of the mountain.
He was fighting for Ireland,
Making things happen. 35
And he told me, Joe Ward,
Of how he had risen through the ranks
To Quartermaster, Commandant:
How every morning at parade
His volunteers would call back *Anseo* 40
And raise their hands
As their names occurred.

GLOSSARY

title *Anseo*: the Irish word for 'present', in answer to a roll call

2 *Collegelands*: an area in Co. Armagh near where the poet was brought up

9 *ledger*: register, roll

10 *Joseph Mary Plunkett Ward*: the boy was clearly called after Joseph Mary Plunkett, executed after the Rising of 1916

13 *droll*: amusing

14 *Ward-of-court*: a play on the phrase 'ward of court', to be in the care of the courts

22 *salley-rod*: a type of stick cut from the salley tree

24 *whittled down to a whip-lash*: pared down until it became like a whip

25 *lacquers*: varnishes

27 *wrought*: made

38 *Quartermaster*: a staff officer in the army (here, the IRA)

GUIDELINES

'Anseo' is from the volume *Why Brownlee Left* (1980). It was written when the Northern Ireland conflict, known as 'The Troubles', seemed to have no solution.

Stanza 1: Irish children have often used the Irish word 'Anseo', meaning 'present', during roll call at school, as the speaker and his classmates did at primary school in Collegelands, Co. Armagh. One of the boys in the class, Joseph Mary Plunkett Ward, was often absent, a fact remarked on sarcastically by the teacher.

The boy's name is significant in the context of Irish history (see annotations above). As the poem is set in Northern Ireland it suggests that his parents' political views were those of the Irish Catholic Nationalists. The reasons why he was absent from school are not explained. Nor are we given any explanation why the 'Master' (schoolteacher) reacted as he did, with his rather feeble pun on the boy's last name.

Stanza 2: The speaker remembers how the teacher would send Joseph Mary Plunkett Ward out to cut a stick with which he would beat him. He describes in an unemotional way how the boy became so used to being beaten that he would arrive at school with the stick already cut. The sticks are described almost as if they were beautiful objects, 'Sanded and polished'. Even the boy himself seems immune to being punished. He has gone so far as to carve his own initials on the stick.

When you read these lines it is easy to gloss over the fact that corporal punishment was an accepted part of school life. Not only that, but to our modern minds it seems incredible that a child would be asked to prepare his own instrument of punishment, as he was. The speaker does not make any comment, underlining perhaps the fact that generations of children did not question the treatment they sometimes got at school.

Stanza 3: These lines suggest that his treatment at school had a profound effect on Joe Ward's later career. We see him as an adult, now a member of the Irish Republican Army, involved in the Northern Ireland conflict known as 'The Troubles'. It is clear that he is now in a position of power over others, as the teacher had once been over him. Ironically, he calls the roll in exactly the same way as the master had in school, so that the volunteers must answer 'Anseo'.

THE THEME OF THE POEM

The poet/speaker makes no direct comment on Joe Ward (as he is now known) or his situation. The connection is clear, though, between the boy's treatment at school and his later life of violence. His experience of being brutalised by the schoolteacher has made him insensitive to the pain of others or the damage his actions may cause. Perhaps this is one of the themes of the poem: what happens to us in childhood affects the way we live later on and what we do. Ironically, though, Joe Ward seems unaware of this. Is this the worst irony of all?

QUESTIONS

1 What impression of primary school life does this poem give us?

2 What aspect of the story do you find most disturbing? Give reasons for your view.

3 Why do you think the poet describes the hazel-wand in such detail in the second stanza?

4 Do you think there is a connection between Joe Ward's early experiences at school and his activities in the IRA? Or is there a more complex reason for his activities? Might it have any connection with his personal circumstances, including the name given to him by his parents? Look again at the first stanza.

5 Which of these words would come closest to describing the tone of the poem, in your opinion: angry, disappointed, bitter, disgusted, detached? Refer to the poem in support of your views.

6 What, in your opinion, is the main point the poem makes? Do you agree with it?

7 Imagine you are one of Joe Ward's 'Volunteers'. Write a short account of the life you lead and say what you think of your leader.

RICHARD MURPHY

B. 1927

BIOGRAPHY

Richard Murphy was born in Galway. His father, Sir William Lindsay Murphy, was in the British Colonial Service, and Murphy spent his childhood in Ceylon and the Bahamas. He attended Oxford and the Sorbonne in Paris. He lived and worked in Crete before returning to Ireland in the early 1960s. He set up home on Inisbofin, making his living from an old sailing boat, which he restored. His 1963 collection, *Sailing to an Island*, won wide acclaim.

In 1985, Murphy's book, *The Price of Stone*, charted his colourful life through the houses and buildings he'd known. The book ranged over his colonial childhood, his English education and his life on a small island. His 1968 book on the Battle of Aughrim is of interest for many reasons, not least because his ancestors fought on both sides.

Murphy's work has always been highly regarded both at home and abroad. Among his most famous literary friends were the poets Ted Hughes and Sylvia Plath. Their visit to him in September 1962, a short time before Plath's death, has received much attention from her biographers.

Richard Murphy now divides his time between Dublin and Durban in South Africa. His *Collected Poems* was published in 2000.

THE READING LESSON

Fourteen years old, learning the alphabet,
He finds letters harder to catch than hares
Without a greyhound. Can't I give him a dog
To track them down, or put them in a cage?
He's caught in a trap, until I let him go,   5
Pinioned by 'Don't you want to learn to read?'
'I'll be the same man whatever I do.'

He looks at a page as a mule balks at a gap
From which a goat may hobble out and bleat.
His eyes jink from a sentence like flushed snipe   10
Escaping shot. A sharp word, and he'll mooch
Back to his piebald mare and bantam cock.
Our purpose is as tricky to retrieve
As mercury from a smashed thermometer.

'I'll not read any more.' Should I give up?   15
His hands, long-fingered as a Celtic scribe's,
Will grow callous, gathering sticks or scrap;
Exploring pockets of the horny drunk
Loiterers at the fairs, giving them lice.
A neighbour chuckles. 'You can never tame   20
The wild duck: when his wings grow, he'll fly off.'

If books resembled roads, he'd quickly read:
But they're small farms to him, fenced by the page,
Ploughed into lines, with letters drilled like oats:
A field of tasks he'll always be outside.   25
If words were bank notes, he would filch a wad;
If they were pheasants, they'd be in his pot
For breakfast, or if wrens he'd make them king.

GLOSSARY

   8 *balks*: hesitates, refuses to go on

  10 *jink*: dodge or move away

  11 *mooch*: move in a half-hearted way

  16 *scribe*: a person, usually a monk, who made copies of books. The Book of Kells was made by scribes

16–17 *a Celtic scribe's…sticks or scraps*: a remarkable feature of the poem is the way in which sounds are repeated and echoed across lines and stanzas, as in the tradition of poetry written in Irish

  17 *callous*: hardened and thick-skinned

  26 *filch*: steal, pilfer

GUIDELINES

The speaker of the poem describes giving a reading lesson to a 14 year-old boy. The poem uses a series of colourful images to suggest the boy's difficulty in mastering letters and words. The images are drawn from the boy's world.

The first line establishes the dramatic situation. The lesson is for a boy, who is almost a man in the Traveller culture to which he belongs, but who has not yet learned to read. The first line also establishes the style of the poem. It is written in lines of ten syllables, the traditional line length for poets writing in English, going back to the time of Shakespeare. However, the poem imitates some of the sound patterns of poetry written in Irish, thereby combining both an Irish and an English tradition of poetry.

In lines 2 and 3, the narrator introduces the first of many comparisons that describe what the boy cannot do by drawing attention to the things he can do. The boy feels trapped in the reading lesson. However, for the teacher, reading is a form of freedom. The final line of the first stanza, 'I'll be the same man whatever I do', illustrates the boy's pride, defiance and, perhaps, his vulnerability.

In the second stanza the comparison of the boy to a mule suggests the boy's awkward, stubborn, possibly belligerent attitude to the task of learning to read. The narrator continues to describe the boy's reaction to reading with images taken from the boy's world in which animals play a large part.

The reference to the scribe in Stanza 3 is a reminder that the Travellers are inheritors of the Celtic tradition. Perhaps it suggests that the loss of reading and writing is a loss of the boy's birthright? The comment of the neighbour, 'You can never tame / The wild duck: when his wings grow, he'll fly off,' raises the question of whether the teacher is trying to turn the boy into something that he is not. However, the motivation of the teacher can be interpreted as a desire to save the boy from the rough, dirty life that lies ahead of him.

There is a change of tone in the final stanza. The teacher seems to have abandoned his or her efforts to teach the boy. The stanza is composed of a series of 'If only' statements which express regret at the failure to help the boy to read while speaking affectionately of him. The final image concludes the poem on a note of celebration and flight.

QUESTIONS

1 In the first stanza the speaker compares the boy's difficulty in reading to catching hares without a greyhound. In the context of the poem, is this a good image?

2 What, do you think, is the tone of the boy's remark, 'I'll be the same man whatever I do.' What does this line reveal to us about the boy?

3 What comparisons (similes) are used in Stanza 2 to describe the way the boy looks at the page? What do they tell us about the boy?

4 a) What makes the job of teaching the boy so 'tricky'?
   b) What is the neighbour's attitude to the reading lesson (lines 20–21)?

5 What future does the speaker foresee for the boy (lines 16–19)?

6 'A field of tasks he'll always be outside' (line 25). The last stanza tells us much about the boy's world and way of life. Write a short piece describing this life, incorporating all the information given in the stanza.

7 Select three words, phrases or images that you like most in the poem. Explain your choice.

8 Take a stanza and count the number of syllables in each line. Examine the rhymes/half rhymes used by the poet. Look at any two lines and comment on the sounds in the lines and their effect.

9 'Should I give up?' (line 15). By the end of the poem, do you think the teacher has given up? Explain your answer.

10 It has been said that in his poetry Richard Murphy often celebrates people who are outsiders. Is the boy in this poem an outsider? Explain your answer.

HOWARD NEMEROV

1920–1991

BIOGRAPHY

Howard Nemerov was born into a wealthy Jewish family on 29 February 1920 in New York City. His parents owned a fashionable department store on Fifth Avenue. Both his father and mother were interested in art and theatre. Nemerov had two sisters. Diane became a celebrated photographer and Renee became a sculptor. The young Nemerov grew up in a privileged home. The family had two maids, a cook, a chauffeur and a German nanny. The family was untouched by the 1929 stock market crash and the Great Depression.

Nemerov attended a private school and was an excellent student who enjoyed sports. Graduating from high school in 1937, Nemerov was accepted into Harvard University and earned a Bachelor of Arts degree in English. After college, he joined an American unit of the Canadian Air Force, earning the rank of first lieutenant. He flew combat missions during the Second World War. In 1944 Nemerov married and after the war he and his wife moved to New York. Those who knew him describe Howard Nemerov as a witty companion.

Nemerov published his first book of poetry in 1947 and a novel soon followed. In all, during his long career he published thirteen books of poetry, three novels, short stories and literary criticism. His final collection of poetry was published shortly after his death in 1991. He also had a career as a university teacher of literature.

Nemerov won many awards and prizes for his writing, including the Pulitzer Prize and the National Book Award. He was also the Poet Laureate for the Library of Congress in America from 1988 to 1990, a position given in recognition of outstanding achievement in poetry. The Poet Laureate gives a series of lectures and writes poems for State occasions, such as the inauguration of the President. Despite these honours and awards Nemerov, an intensely private man, remained insecure about his achievement as a writer.

As a poet, Nemerov is known for his intelligence, wit and irreverence. His friend and fellow poet, James Dickey said of him:

> Nemerov is a poet of great wit and deep resources. He's the most unboring poet I know. He can say funny and serious things at the same time, and is the best of both wit and seriousness we have now.

Of his own poetry, Nemerov remarked:

> I do insist on making what I hope is sense so there's always a coherent narrative or argument that the reader can follow instantly the first time through and then if there's something more to occupy the reader, I've been lucky.

Howard Nemerov died of throat cancer in 1991.

WOLVES IN THE ZOO

They look like big dogs badly drawn, drawn wrong.
A legend on their cage tells us there is
No evidence that any of their kind
Has ever attacked man, woman, or child.

Now it turns out there were no babies dropped   5
In sacrifice, delaying tactics, from
Siberian sleds; now it turns out, so late,
That Little Red Ridinghood and her Gran

Were the aggressors with the slavering fangs
And tell-tale tails; now it turns out at last   10
That grey wolf and timber wolf are near extinct,
Done out of being by the tales we tell

Told us by Nanny in the nursery;
Young sparks we were, to set such forest fires
As blazed from story into history   15
And put such bounty on their wolvish heads

As brought the few survivors to our terms,
Surrendered in happy Babylon among
The peacock dusting off the path of dust,
The tiger pacing in the striped shade.   20

GLOSSARY

2 *legend*: in this context, information and explanation. The word also means a traditional story or a popular belief. The poem contrasts the 'scientific' information given about wolves with the beliefs expressed in stories and fairy-tales

7 *Siberian sleds*: Siberia is a vast area of land in Northern Russia. Traditionally, many of the native people were nomadic, living off hunting and fishing. Because the winters are harsh and cold, and because a large portion of the territory is within the Arctic, sleds were a common form of transport. There are many tales of nomadic people sacrificing the frailest member of their group so that the others might survive. The Siberian wolf is famed for its resourcefulness in surviving in a harsh wilderness. In Mongolian mythology (Mongolia borders Siberia), Genghis Khan is said to have descended from a wolf

9 *the slavering fangs*: with saliva running from the long, sharp teeth. 'Slavering fangs' suggests that the teeth are moist in greedy anticipation of the feast to come.

10 *grey wolf and timber wolf*: the grey wolf is the most common species of wolf, with a distribution across North America, Europe and Northern Asia. The timber wolf is a subspecies of the grey wolf, found in North America

16 *bounty*: money paid as a reward. Many governments (or wealthy farmers) paid a bounty to hunters for every wolf that they killed. The first wolf bounty was introduced into the United States in 1630. There was widespread fear of wolves in Europe in the Middle Ages and European settlers brought this fear with them to America

17 *our terms*: the imagery suggests a war, in which the defeated survivors, the wolves, accept the terms of surrender

18 *Babylon*: an ancient city in what is now known as Iraq. The city was the centre of a kingdom that was bounded by two great rivers, the Tigris and the Euphrates. Along these two rivers were many trading cities such as Ur, Ninevah and Babylon itself. The Hanging Gardens of Babylon were one of the wonders of the ancient world. It was reputed to be a place of fruits and flowers, rivers and waterfalls, exotic plants and animals. In many ways, it was a forerunner of the modern zoo. The kingdom of Babylon played an important part in Jewish history. For seventy years (586–516 BC) the Jews lived in captivity in Babylonia. The Jews accepted the exile as a punishment from God ('For because of the anger of the Lord this happened in Jerusalem and Judah, that He finally cast them out from His presence'. *Kings* 2, 24:20), and lived quietly without complaint. The Jewish exiles were allowed to live together in communities, farm along the Euphrates and earn income from other kinds of work.

GUIDELINES

'The wolf at the door', 'to cry wolf,' 'don't wolf down your food,' 'a wolf in sheep's clothing' popular attitudes to the wolf are expressed in many everyday sayings and in well-known stories and legends. In *Little Red Riding Hood* and *The Three Little Pigs*, the wolf is greedy and cruel. The wolves howling in the forests around the castle of Dracula symbolise everything that humans fear about the dark. In the Middle Ages, some humans were thought to be able to transform themselves into wolves. These werewolves were considered to be the servants of the devil. Nemerov's poem contrasts the view of the wolf in legend and folklore with the tame version offered by the 'legend' on the wolves cage in the zoo.

The wolves in the zoo hardly look like wolves, they look like dogs, 'badly drawn'. They accept their new conditions, their new surroundings in 'happy Babylon'. Here the wild animals almost lose their identity. The peacock's tail dusts the path; the tiger seems to have lost its stripes.

The wolves are not really the centre of attention in the poem. Nemerov is more interested in playfully teasing out the difference between the old and the new view of wolves, between science and legend. He takes delight in suggesting that Granny and Little Red Riding Hood were the real aggressors. He is amused by the idea that the tales told by 'Nanny in the nursery' have been the ruination of wolves. There seems to be more scepticism than guilt in the statement, 'Young sparks we were, to set such forest fires / As blazed from story into history'. The poem bears comparison to Sylvia Plath's 'The Times Are Tidy' with the distinction between the modern world and the world of myth and fairy-tale.

With a lightness of touch, the poem questions the nature of truth and the difference between science and folklore. The tone is sceptical and playful.

The poem is written in blank verse, that is, in unrhymed lines of ten syllables. This was the style used by Shakespeare in writing his plays. While the poem is unrhymed, it does contain half-rhymes and many examples of sound and wordplay, in phrases such as 'tell-tale tails', or in 'story into history'.

QUESTIONS

1 Does the poet believe what the legend on the cage says about wolves? Do you believe it? Explain your answer. Support the points you make by quotation from the poem.

2 The phrase, 'Now it turns out...', is used three times in the poem. In what tone(s) of voice should this phrase be recited? Give reasons for your answer.

3 Does the poem make you feel sad for the wolves in the zoo? Explain your point of view.

4 Select two phrases from the poem that you really like. Explain your choice.

5 'There's more to truth than the facts.' Do you think this is what the poem is saying? Support the points you make by quotation from the poem.

6 What impression of the poet do you form from the poem? Refer to the poem in your answer.

7 'He can say funny and serious things at the same time.' Is 'Wolves in the Zoo' an example of Howard Nemerov saying funny and serious things at the same time?

SHARON OLDS

B. 1942

BIOGRAPHY

Sharon Olds was born in 1942 in San Francisco. She was educated at Stanford University and Columbia University. Her first book of poems, *Satan Says* (1980), received the San Francisco Poetry Center Award, while her second book, *The Dead and the Living* (1983) was the winner of the National Book Critics' Circle Award. Her other poetry collections include *The Gold Cell*, *The Father*, *The Wellspring* and *Blood, Tin, Straw*.

Sharon Olds has been writer-in-residence at a number of academic institutions in the USA. In recent years she has taught poetry workshops in the Graduate Program in Creative Writing at New York University and in the NYU workshop at Goldwater Hospital for the severely disabled in New York. She was appointed New York State Poet for 1998–2000.

THE PRESENT MOMENT

Now that he cannot sit up,
now that he just lies there
looking at the wall, I forget the one
who sat up and put on his reading glasses
and the lights in the room multiplied in the lenses.   5
Once he entered the hospital
I forgot the man who lay full length
on the couch, with the blanket folded around him,
that huge, crushed bud, and I have
long forgotten the man who ate food—   10
not dense, earthen food, like liver, but
things like pineapple, wedges of light,
the skeiny nature of light made visible.
It's as if I abandoned that ruddy man
with the swollen puckered mouth of a sweet-eater,   15
the torso packed with extra matter
like a planet a handful of which weighs as much as the earth, I have
left behind forever that young man my father,
that smooth-skinned, dark-haired boy,
and my father long before I knew him, when he could   20
only sleep, or drink from a woman's
body, a baby who stared with a steady
gaze the way he lies there, now, with his
eyes open, then the lids start down
and the milky crescent of the other world   25
shines, in there, for a moment, before sleep.
I stay beside him, like someone in a rowboat
staying abreast of a Channel swimmer,
you are not allowed to touch them, their limbs
glow, faintly, in the night water.   30

11 *earthen*: solid

13 *skeiny*: web-like

14 *ruddy*: red-faced

16 *torso*: upper part of the body

25 *crescent*: curved shape, like the waning moon

28 *Channel swimmer*: someone who swims the Channel to compete or set a record

GUIDELINES

'The Present Moment' is from the collection *The Father* (1992), a sequence of poems dealing with a daughter's experience of her father's illness and death. Many of the poems, like this one, are quite disturbing as they express the speaker's attempts to come to terms with a relationship that was at times difficult and painful.

The poem begins with a painful and moving image of her father lying helpless in the last days of his life, in the present moment. Now that he can do very little for himself, she admits that it is hard to remember him as he used to be.

The poem moves backwards in time to visualise the man as he was. Each different stage is recreated in vivid details, carefully selected to give a good impression of the man he was. Although the speaker says more than once that she has 'forgotten' what he was like before he became ill, we actually get the opposite impression. All the different phases of his life have been etched in her memory. She even goes so far as to imagine what he might have been like as a baby.

She sees him as he was just before he went into hospital, lying on a couch, once a big strong man, now a 'crushed bud'. Once he 'ate food' (the image is disturbing, since food is so important to us all). She gives us an idea of the sheer physical presence of the man as he once was, someone who clearly loomed large in the life of his daughter. A psychologist might examine some of the images here with interest, as she compares him to a 'planet', as someone who had an extraordinary power over his daughter.

She moves further back into his life, so that we see him as a young man, and even further, as a baby at his mother's breast, as helpless then as he is now. It is as if the newness of the baby, so close still to the other world of the womb, and the closeness to death of the older man, are alike in some way. The word 'shines' links the image with other images of light throughout the poem.

In the last lines the poet tells us how she supports him in his last illness. Like a 'Channel swimmer' he must struggle on alone. But there is tenderness and beauty in the last image of limbs that 'glow' in the night water, or in the final moments of life.

You will notice that the poem is arranged as one long stanza. Most of the lines do not finish with a full stop, but run on to the next line as in one long sentence. The impression this gives is one of rapid movement, which fits in with the poet's depiction of her father's life as a journey.

QUESTIONS

1 From line 1 to line 26 the poem moves backwards from images of the father as he is now to images of him as a baby. Explore each image carefully and suggest which aspect of the father's personality it reveals.

2 Which image do you find the most interesting or puzzling?

3 What is your overall impression of the speaker's father as he is described in the poem? Do you think he is a likeable man?

4 What sort of relationship does the speaker have with her father, in your opinion?

5 Why do you think Sharon Olds wrote this poem?

6 Which of the following statements comes closest to describing the speaker's attitude to the situation in the poem, in your view:

■ the speaker is upset and sad at her father's illness
■ the speaker is puzzled by the mystery of illness and death
■ the speaker feels helpless in the face of her father's illness.

Perhaps you have another suggestion to make?

7 Do you find this poem disturbing, moving, painful to read? Perhaps you had another response entirely?

SYLVIA PLATH

1932–1963

BIOGRAPHY

Sylvia Plath was born in a seaside suburb of Boston in 1932. Both her parents, Otto Plath and Aurelia Schober, were academics and had German ancestry. They believed in the virtues of hard work and were committed to education. Sylvia was a bright, intelligent child and won many school prizes and awards.

When Sylvia was eight, her father fell ill. Convinced that he had cancer, he refused to attend a doctor. When, eventually, a diagnosis was confirmed, he had to undergo an operation to amputate his leg. He died shortly afterwards. When Sylvia learned of his death, she declared, 'I'll never speak to God again'. Anxious to spare Sylvia and her younger brother Warren any unnecessary upset, their mother did not bring them to the funeral. Her father's death haunted Sylvia for the remainder of her life.

Otto Plath's death left the family in difficult financial circumstances. Aurelia Plath took up a full-time teaching job to support her children and Sylvia's grandparents moved in with the family in a house in the prosperous suburb of Wellesley. Later Sylvia wrote that the move to Wellesley marked the end of her idyllic childhood by the sea.

All through High School, Plath published poems and stories in local and national newspapers and in her school magazine. In her final year at school,

Seventeen, a national teen magazine, published her short story 'And Summer Will Not Come Again'. It was an important landmark in the young writer's life.

In 1951, Plath entered Smith College, an exclusive women's college in Massachusetts, with the help of two scholarships. Plath's first two years at Smith went well. Her talent and intelligence were nurtured by the teaching staff, her grades were excellent and she continued to have her work published. During her second year at Smith, she was awarded a fiction prize by *Mademoiselle,* a fashionable, upmarket magazine for young women. During this period she dated Dick Norton, a childhood friend from Wellesley who came from a wealthy background.

Despite these successes, academic, personal and social, Plath was deeply insecure about herself. The beginning of her third year in college saw her beset by many doubts and uncertainties. A four-week guest editorship at *Mademoiselle* in New York did little to improve matters. Failure to secure a place on a summer course run by Frank O'Connor at Harvard in 1953 caused a crisis, and she was sent for psychiatric treatment. A poorly supervised and administered series of electric shock treatments worsened her condition and she made an attempt to take her own life. She was missing for three days, unconscious in a narrow space under the family home. She recovered her health over a period of six months with the help of a sympathetic psychiatrist.

Smith College offered her a scholarship to allow her to finish her degree, and she returned to the college in spring 1954, graduating with distinction. By now she had acquired a growing reputation as a writer.

More success came her way in the form of a prestigious Fulbright scholarship to study at Cambridge University. She entered Newnham College in October 1955. It was in Cambridge that Sylvia Plath met the poet Ted Hughes. After a whirlwind romance, the couple married on Bloomsday, June 16, 1956. Plath returned to Cambridge to complete her studies in Autumn 1956, continuing all the while to write. At the same time she helped Hughes organise and send out his work. ('Black Rook in Rainy Weather' was written in this period.) The couple moved to America in summer 1957, and Plath taught for a year at Smith. She found the job taxing and considered herself to be a poor teacher. While Hughes continued to enjoy publishing success, Plath found it impossible to find time to devote to her writing in the way that she longed. At the end of the academic year in summer 1958, Plath resigned her teaching position at Smith, against her mother's wishes, and the couple rented a small apartment in Boston. The year was not without its difficulties. Plath suffered from writer's block and depression. 'The Times Are Tidy' was one of the few poems she completed. She was worried by financial concerns and tried to supplement their income by taking part-time secretarial work. By summer 1959, things had improved. Hughes continued to write and publish and Plath, too, completed both poems and short stories. The couple then decided to return to England. Before they left America, they spent two months at a writer's colony in New York State. Relieved of domestic duties, Plath wrote freely and finished a number of the poems that are included in *The Colossus*, the only collection published during her lifetime.

Frieda Rebecca Hughes, the couple's first child, was born in April 1960 in London. By this time, Heinemann had agreed to publish *The Colossus* and Hughes had won the prestigious Somerset Maughan Award. Plath, however, was disappointed by the lack of reaction to *The Colossus*, and while she loved her husband and new daughter, she found that the roles of mother and wife took her away from her writing.

The year 1961 was a topsy-turvy one for Sylvia Plath. It began with the sadness of a miscarriage, followed by an operation to remove an appendix. Her recovery from this she likened to a resurrection. A contract with the *New Yorker* magazine boosted her morale and she began work on her novel, *The Bell Jar*. When Plath became pregnant the couple decided to look for a house in the country, eventually moving in the autumn to Court Green in Devon. This was a rambling, crumbling old house with three acres of lawn, garden and orchard. Despite her pregnancy, the care of a young daughter and the practicalities of setting up home in an old house, Plath wrote with great energy in the first months in Devon, though the poems she completed, including 'Finisterre' and 'Mirror', are marked by a sense of threat, fear and menace.

In January 1962, Plath gave birth to her second child, Nicholas. Her experience of birth and her remembrance of her miscarriage in the previous year inform the radio play, *Three Women*, that she wrote for the BBC in the spring of 1962. The poems written later in 1962, most notably 'Elm', are dark meditations on love and self-knowledge.

By summer 1962 Plath's marriage to Hughes was beginning to unravel. Hughes became involved with Assia Wevill, the wife of a Canadian poet, and left Court Green. A holiday in Ireland in September failed to save the relationship.

Back in Court Green in October and November, Sylvia Plath, working early in the morning, wrote forty of the poems that make up the collection *Ariel*, including 'Poppies in July' and 'The Arrival of the Bee Box', published after her death. By any standards, these are remarkable poems. Writing to a friend, she said, 'I am living like a Spartan, writing through huge fevers and producing free stuff I had locked in me for years'. The strain of writing these intense, personal poems began to affect her health. Her letters to her mother from this period are touched with desperation. In November Plath decided to move back to London and found a flat in the house where W. B. Yeats had once lived. By December she had closed up Court Green and moved into her new home with her two young children. In the New Year, some of the worst weather seen in London for decades, allied to the delay in obtaining a phone and the colds and flu she and the children suffered, cast her down and left her feeling isolated. She was further disheartened by the fact that her new work was, on the whole, rejected by the editors to whom she sent it. The publication of her novel, *The Bell Jar*, under a pseudonym, did little to lift the gloom. Her final poems (including 'Child'), written in late January and early February, reveal that her will to live was almost spent. At this point Sylvia Plath sought medical help and was put on a course of anti-depressants and arrangements were made for her to see a psychiatrist. However, in the early hours of Monday morning, February 11, 1963, overcome by a despairing depression, Sylvia Plath took her own life.

Ariel, a collection of her final poems was published in 1965. Since that time, it has sold over half a million copies. Sylvia Plath's life, death and poetry have been the subject of much controversy. Understandably, given the tragic circumstances of her death, much of the response to her poetry has sought to relate her work to her life – to find clues in her poetry to explain her suicide or to attribute blame. The difference between the personality that Sylvia Plath reveals in her letters home to her mother and the darker personality of her journals has also attracted the attention of critics. Rarely has a poet left such a disputed body of work.

THE ARRIVAL OF THE BEE BOX

I ordered this, this clean wood box
Square as a chair and almost too heavy to lift.
I would say it was the coffin of a midget
Or a square baby
Were there not such a din in it.   5

The box is locked, it is dangerous.
I have to live with it overnight
And I can't keep away from it.
There are no windows, so I can't see what is in there.
There is only a little grid, no exit.   10

I put my eye to the grid.
It is dark, dark,
With the swarmy feeling of African hands
Minute and shrunk for export,
Black on black, angrily clambering.   15

How can I let them out?
It is the noise that appals me most of all,
The unintelligible syllables.
It is like a Roman mob,
Small, taken one by one, but my god, together!   20

I lay my ear to furious Latin.
I am not a Caesar.
I have simply ordered a box of maniacs.
They can be sent back.
They can die, I need feed them nothing, I am the owner.   25

I wonder how hungry they are.
I wonder if they would forget me
If I just undid the locks and stood back and turned into a tree.
There is the laburnum, its blond colonnades,
And the petticoats of the cherry.   30

They might ignore me immediately
In my moon suit and funeral veil.
I am no source of honey
So why should they turn on me?
Tomorrow I will be sweet God, I will set them free.   35

The box is only temporary.

GLOSSARY

13–14 *the swarmy feeling …export*: Plath was influenced by the surrealist painter Giorgio de Chirico, and his use of symbols taken from the subconscious to create ominous, disturbing images. She was also interested in African sculpture and folktales. Both interests, surrealism and Africa, come together in the imagery of the stanza

19 *a Roman mob*: the Roman mob demanded public killings for their amusement. The comparison suggests the potential for destruction that the speaker senses in the bee box

29 *blond colonnades*: the flower-covered branches of the laburnum are compared to blond ringlets

30 *my moon suit and funeral veil*: Plath compares the protective suit worn by bee-keepers to the suit of an astronaut, while she associates the veil with the traditional veil worn by women mourners at a funeral

GUIDELINES

In summer 1962, Sylvia Plath and Ted Hughes decided to take up bee-keeping. (Plath's father had been an expert on bees.) In October, following her separation from Ted Hughes, Plath wrote a sequence of bee poems which explore the nature of the self and self-identity, personal fears, complex relations and attitudes towards freedom and control. Of the five poems in the sequence, 'The Arrival of the Bee Box' is the most self-contained and narrative. The poem may be taken at face value – it describes the arrival of the bee box and the poet's response to it.

However, the bee box is sometimes interpreted as a metaphor for the inner life of the poet.

The bee box, and all it represents, both frightens and attracts the speaker of the poem, who is fascinated with its unknown and dangerous content. As the poem progresses, the persona grows confident and determines to set the bees free. She is still fearful of what they might do and fearful, perhaps, that in freeing the bees she may lose something vital. However, if the persona risks losing something, she also has something to gain – the feeling of exercising her power in a generous way. There is a note of optimistic triumph in the final line of the poem.

If the bee box is a metaphor for what Carol Ferrier describes as 'the fertile, swarming and potentially destructive chaos that the poet sense within herself', how do we interpret the ending of the poem? Is the persona facing up to her own fears and finding a strength of purpose and resolve? Does the ending of the poem suggest that she will control her fears rather than allow her fears to control her? However, if the bees represent the inner life of the poetic persona, then the box may represent the body which contains it. 'The box is only temporary' may suggest that the inner life will be freed when it is released from the containing body – when the body dies. If the end of the poem suggests liberation, the precise nature of the liberation is unclear.

David Holbrook gives this interesting reading of the poem:

In 'The Arrival of the Bee Box' Sylvia Plath achieves a significantly developed sense of distinction between herself and the bees – she discovers resources in herself by which to deal with reality, to care for the bees, as for children. The poem's images are of a rebirth, beginning with a dead baby, ending with free bees, and the escape from death. By her recognition of the bees not merely as aspects of her identity, but as creatures in themselves, she, as 'sweet God', can release them to be themselves (as in the end she released her children).

QUESTIONS

1 Do you find the imagery of the first stanza strange, disturbing, amusing? Explain your answer.

2 'In line 7, "I have to live with it overnight", we see that the bee box represents the speaker's unconscious and is linked to the imagery of 'the dark thing that sleeps in me', referred to by the speaker in "Elm".' Do you agree with this reading of the line? Support the points you make by reference to the poem.

3 What impression is created of the box and its contents in Stanzas 3–4? What phrase or image strikes you as particularly effective?

4 In Stanza 5, the speaker seems to gain a sense of control over the box. What brings this about? What change of heart is apparent in Stanza 6?

5 In Stanzas 6–7, the speaker contemplates her own self-effacement as a way of avoiding the threat of the bees. What does this suggest about the speaker?

6 'Tomorrow I will be sweet God, I will set them free' (line 35). What is the importance of this line in the poem, and what impact does it have on you?

7 'In the poem, there is both a desire to trust the bees and a fear of trusting them, but in the end, the fear is overcome.' Do you agree with this reading of the poem? Explain your answer.

8 'The poem is remarkable for its humour; the confident handling of language; and its stanza form and organisation.' In light of this statement, comment on the form and language of the poem.

9 The critic Carole Ferrier says that: 'In this poem the box of bees becomes a metaphor for the fertile, swarming, and potentially destructive chaos that the poet senses within herself'. Comment on this assessment of the poem and the assumption that the persona of the poem is the poet.

10 In your view does the poem end on a note of optimism? Explain your answer.

CHILD

Your clear eye is the one absolutely beautiful thing.
I want to fill it with colour and ducks.
The zoo of the new

Whose names you meditate—
April snowdrop, Indian pipe,   5
Little

Stalk without wrinkle,
Pool in which images
Should be grand and classical

Not this troublous   10
Wringing of hands, this dark
Ceiling without a star.

GLOSSARY

title *Child*: Sylvia Plath's second child, Nicholas, was born in January 1962. 'Child' was
  written shortly after his first birthday and less than two weeks before her death

  4 *meditate*: the word means 'to reflect upon' and is used to pick up the imagery of
    reflection begun in line 1, 'clear eye' and continued in line 8 with 'Pool'

  5 *snowdrop*: small, white-flowering plant that blooms in spring

  5 *Indian pipe*: small woodland flower

  10 *troublous*: taking up the idea of classical and grand in the preceding line, Plath
    uses an old-fashioned, literary word, which means agitated or unsettled

GUIDELINES

'Child' appeared in Plath's posthumous collection 'Winter Trees', published in
1971, although it was written at the end of January 1963, less than two weeks
before she took her own life at the age of thirty. The poetic persona expresses her
frustrated wishes for her child. The poem is beautifully phrased and composed.

The mother wants her child's eye to be filled with delightful things. She would like his eye to be filled with images that are 'grand and classical'. However, what he witnesses is the classical gesture of despair – the wringing of hands by his mother. This gesture is both troubled and troubling. In the poem, the power of the self is reduced to expressing its own anguish. The mother inhabits a world without hope. Her failure to fill the child's world with joy adds to her darkness and distress.

It is difficult not to read this poem in the biographical context in which it was written – two weeks before Sylvia Plath took her own life. The self that the poem presents is a self that has lost confidence in its own ability to create joy. It is a self that is shadowed by its own anguish. The mother is aware of her despair and anxious to spare her child the sight of it. The mother does not want the child's clear eye to witness the pain she endures, yet lacks the strength and self-belief – not the humour, imagination or inventiveness – to make things otherwise.

'Child' is a testimony to Sylvia Plath's skill as a poet. Every word is carefully chosen. The placing of 'Little' (line 6) and 'dark' (line 11) is perfectly judged. The despair that underlies it is managed and controlled. 'Poppies in July' and 'Mirror' also present a persona who is tormented and anguished.

QUESTIONS

1 How does the mother regard her child in line 1? What is the significance of describing the child's eye as 'clear'?

2 What does line 1 tell us about the world that the poetic persona inhabits?

3 What wish does the mother express in lines 2–3? What ideas and mood are generated by the use of the word 'zoo'?

4 What is the effect of the names recited by the mother? In what sense might the child 'meditate' the names? What is the relationship between the names and the child, in the mother's world?

5 What are the conditions in which the images in a pool might appear 'grand and classical'? Do these conditions exist in the child's life?

6 What does Stanza 4 tell us about the mother? What feeling does the mother have in relation to her child? What feeling do you have for the mother?

7 'As with all Plath's poetry, "Child" reveals her mastery of movement and phrasing.' Give your view of this assessment of the poem.

8 '"Child" can be placed with "Mirror" and "Poppies in July" in presenting an individual in tormented anguish.' Give your view of this interpretation of the poem, supporting the points you make by quotation from the poem.

CHRISTINA GEORGINA ROSSETTI

1830–1894

BIOGRAPHY

Christina Rossetti was a member of one of the most famous families in Victorian England. Her father was the poet Gabriele Rossetti (1783–1854), professor of Italian at King's College from 1831. All the four children in the family became writers. Her brother, Dante Gabriel, also gained fame as a painter. Christina was educated at home by her mother, Frances Polidori, an intelligent woman, who was a devout Anglican. Christina shared her parents' interest in literature and was portrayed in the paintings and drawings of her brother and his friends. Based on the sketches made by her brother the young Christina was an attractive, even beautiful, woman.

When Gabriele Rossetti's failing health and eyesight forced him into retirement in 1853, Christina and her mother attempted to support the family by starting a day school, but had to give it up after a year or so. Like her mother, Christina was a devout Anglican and rejected two offers of marriage because of religious differences. Except for two brief visits abroad, she lived with her mother all her life.

After a serious illness in 1874, and recurrent bouts of Graves' disease, a disorder of the thyroid which altered her appearance, she rarely went outside her home. However, her circle of friends included some of the most important writers and artists of the day, including Whistler, Swinburne and Charles Dodgson (Lewis Carroll). Christina's religious feelings influenced how she led her life. For example, she gave up playing chess because she found she enjoyed winning too much!

She felt keenly the death of her beloved brother, Dante, in 1882 and, although she survived him by twelve years, she lived quietly, beset by bouts of ill health. In the weeks preceding her death, she disturbed her neighbours each night with her terrible screams of agony. Christina Rossetti died on December 29, 1894.

Christina Rossetti was composing stories and poems from before she could write, dictating her compositions to her mother. Her first collection of poetry was published in 1862, and was widely praised. It established her as a significant and distinctive voice in Victorian poetry. Several books followed: love poems and religious verse for adults, poetry and short stories for children. She wrote the words for the Christmas carol 'In the bleak midwinter' and she wrote pamphlets for the Society for Promoting Christian Knowledge. At its best, Christina Rossetti's poetry is remarkably clear and direct and her handling of form is masterful. Her recurrent themes are unhappy love, death and renunciation.

'REMEMBER ME WHEN I AM GONE AWAY'

Remember me when I am gone away,
Gone far away into the silent land;
When you can no more hold me by the hand,
Nor I half turn to go yet turning stay.
Remember me when no more day by day   5
You tell me of our future that you planned:
Only remember me; you understand
It will be late to counsel then or pray.
Yet if you should forget me for a while
And afterwards remember, do not grieve: 10
For if the darkness and corruption leave
A vestige of the thoughts that once I had,
Better by far you should forget and smile
Than that you should remember and be sad.

GLOSSARY

2 *the silent land*: usually taken as a metaphor for death. In the context of the poem as a whole, you might consider other possible meanings of the phrase

8 *counsel*: to give advice; to advise on matters of morality especially in relation to poverty, chastity and obedience

11 *the darkness and corruption*: usually interpreted as death. The speaker is referring to the darkness of her own death and the corruption of her body. However, if the terms 'darkness' and 'corruption' refer to the person she is addressing, then an entirely different reading emerges

12 *A vestige*: a trace; a hint; a slight amount of something that was once plentiful

GUIDELINES

'Remember me' was written in 1849 when Rossetti was just 19 years old. In the poem, a woman addresses her beloved before her death and urges him to remember her, or to forget her, if remembering makes him sad.

It is unwise to identify the speaker in the poem with the poet. This, in common with other poems that Rossetti wrote at this time, is a dramatic monologue. The most notable feature of the poem is the ambivalence which the speaker reveals towards the person she addresses. For some readers, the poem is marked by an unexpected irony and a note of anger. The speaker may well welcome death as a release from the lover's grasp and insensitivity, from the future that *he* planned for them both. This reading is dependent upon the tone in which certain key lines and phrases are read. Lines 3–4, 6, 8 and 11 are all open to different interpretations.

The dramatic situation (the speaker addressing her beloved before her death) is reminiscent of the poetry of Emily Dickinson. In 'After Death', another poem which Rossetti wrote in 1849, the speaker lies on a bed with a shroud on her face, observing the surroundings before her burial. It has a similar ambivalent quality to 'Remember me': 'He did not love me living; but once dead / He pitied me; and very sweet it is / To know he still is warm tho' I am cold.'

'Remember me' has little of the passionate declarations of love associated with Victorian love poetry. Instead it has a clarity and directness, an unsentimental, clear-eyed detachment that suggests that, for the speaker, her feelings of love have cooled, if not disappeared. Some traditional views of Rossetti have described her poetry as sincere and superficial. Recent criticism by feminist scholars suggest that Rossetti's poetry is far more subtle in its effects and intentions than has been understood or appreciated. 'Remember me', for example, is based on a paradox. The poem begins with an invitation to remember and concludes with an exhortation to forget!

'Remember me' is remarkable for the ease with which Rossetti rhymes and makes the thought fit the sonnet shape, while maintaining a dramatic voice, which gives the poem a contemporary feel.

Virigina Woolf's estimation of Christina Rossetti as a poet may help in reading 'Remember me':

> You were not a pure saint by any means. You pulled legs; you tweaked noses. You were at war with all humbug and pretense. Modest as you were, still you were drastic, sure of your gift, convinced of your vision … in a word, you were an artist.

The speaker of the poem may well share Rossetti's impatience with pretence and though she speaks simply and directly, there is a strength and confidence in her voice.

QUESTIONS

1 What is the speaker of the poem asking the 'you' to do after her death?

2 How does the speaker feel about the 'you' of the poem? What lines best reveal her feelings?

3 'It will be late to counsel then or pray.' What impression of the 'you' do you form from this line? Explain your answer. Where else do you think the character of the 'you' is suggested?

4 Describe a dramatic situation which you think fits the poem. Give a description of the speaker and the 'you' to whom she addresses her words.

5 Prepare two readings of the poem which offer contrasting views of the relationship between the speaker of the poem and the 'you'.

6 The poem has a number of opposites or contrasts. Identify these and comment on them.

7 What is your impression of the speaker of the poem? Support the points you make by quotation form the poem.

8 Is 'Remember me' a well-made poem? Support the points you make by quotation from the poem.

9 Do you like the poem? Explain your answer.

EDWARD THOMAS

1878–1917

BIOGRAPHY

Edward Thomas was born in London to Welsh parents. He was educated at Oxford and married while still an undergraduate there. His early reputation was made as a prose writer. He wrote a number of enjoyable nature studies, among them *The South Country* and *The Heart of England*. It was not until 1914, when he met the American poet Robert Frost who was living in England, that he began writing poems. His first published poems appeared under the pseudonym of Edward Eastaway in an anthology he edited in 1915. His collected poems were published posthumously in 1918. His poems feature the English landscape, rural life, flora and fauna, transience and endurance. Thomas is not a particularly demanding or challenging poet. His entire output as a poet appeared in the two and a half years before he was killed by a German shell at Arras in 1917.

ADLESTROP

Yes, I remember Adlestrop —
The name, because one afternoon
Of heat the express-train drew up there
Unwontedly. It was late June.

The steam hissed. Someone cleared his throat   5
No one left and no one came
On the bare platform. What I saw
Was Adlestrop — only the name.

And willows, willow-herb, and grass
And meadowsweet, and haycocks dry,   10
Not whit less still and lonely fair
Than the high cloudlets in the sky.

And for that minute a blackbird sang
Close by and round him, mistier,
Farther and farther, all the birds   15
Of Oxfordshire and Gloucestershire.

GUIDELINES

This is a famous anthology piece, in which Thomas puts into practice what he has learned from the poetry of Robert Frost: the matter-of-fact tone, the attentiveness to detail and the plain, straightforward language.

This poem represents a rare achievement. Thomas shows how a single event, simply described, can acquire a mysterious and moving significance. The poet describes a few of the circumstances surrounding the halting of the express train at Adlestrop. He does not try to enforce an interpretation of what he describes but leaves each reader free to create a distinctive meaning from what is described and to speculate on the many possibilities the poem suggests and the many questions it raises.

The key words in the poem are 'I remember'. This is made clear in the first line, where the speaker's emphatic 'Yes' underlines the importance to him of the memories evoked by his brief stop at Adlestrop station. He remembers Adlestrop for two main reasons, each of which gives rise to a two-stanza poem within the body of the poem as a whole. The first eight lines may be read as a self-contained poem. Its theme is the mysterious stop made by an express train at the rural station. It is mysterious because we are not told why the train, which normally passes such unimportant places as Adlestrop, draws up there 'Unwontedly' on a late June day. All we know is that the stop is not made to facilitate passengers, since 'No one left and no one came / On the bare platform'. If the poem ended at line 8, it could still be regarded as a self-contained unit: the poet need not have added the next eight lines for the significance of the previous eight to be complete.

Lines 9–16, however, serve to expand the meaning of the first line of the poem, by telling us why, perhaps, the speaker *really* remembers Adlestrop. The wonderful countryside which surrounds the railway-station is far more memorable than the bare platform on a warm afternoon. The country scene is alive with the beauty of sound and sight. The loneliness of the place adds to the splendour of the grass, the trees and the plants, and of the little clouds floating high above. Just as striking is the impression of distance conveyed by the receding waves of birdsong expanding outwards through the counties of Oxfordshire and Gloucestershire.

The two parts of 'Adlestrop' are distinguished from each other in style and tone. The first eight lines are written in plain, unadorned style, closer to what we might expect from a piece of prose than to a conventional 'poetic style'. The rhythms are relaxed, the description is matter-of-fact. 'It was late June', 'No one left and no one came'. By contrast, the final eight lines are explicitly 'poetic' in style. The speaker's celebration of the beauty of the scene is framed in heightened language. The tone of these lines reflects the speaker's sense of the beauty of what he describes. There is nothing in the first eight lines like the following:

> Not a whit less still and lonely fair
> Than the high cloudlets in the sky.

Notice the urgent rhythms of the description of the blackbird singing close by, and 'round him, mistier / Farther and farther all the birds / Of Oxfordshire and Gloucestershire'.

QUESTIONS

1. The poet gives no reason why the train stops at Adlestrop. Compose a story suggesting a possible reason.
2. Why does the poet remember Adlestrop so well?
3. In what ways do the last two stanzas differ from the first two?
4. The poem creates a sense of mystery. How does it do this?
5. Choose what you think is the best stanza in the poem and give reasons for your choice.
6. The poem illustrates the poet's imagination. Give examples.
7. In what ways do the rhythms of the poem contribute to its meaning?
8. In 'Adlestrop', Thomas evokes what he remembers with remarkable clarity. How does he do this?
9. One critic remarked of Thomas that 'he said what is in the poems, and there is no message beyond them'. How can this remark be applied to Adlestrop?
10. Is there a dimension to Adlestrop beyond what is merely described?
11. Does the poem suggest something about common human experience?
12. Comment on the language of the poem and its effectiveness.

HENRY VAUGHAN

1 6 2 2 – 9 5

BIOGRAPHY

Henry Vaughan was born in Wales and studied at Oxford University. Instead of completing his studies, he took up medicine and practised as a physician. He married in about 1646, and when his first wife died seven years later, he married her sister.

In 1650, Vaughan published *Silex Scintillans*, a book of religious and mystical verse written in the manner of Donne, Herbert and other metaphysical poets. Many of the poems in the collection present emblems of humankind's condition as a spiritual being. *Silex Scintillans*, which means 'sparkling flint', appeared in an enlarged edition in 1655. The preface to this edition claims that the poems were inspired by a religious awakening brought on by a severe illness and by Vaughan's reading of George Herbert's poetry. All of Vaughan's poetic masterpieces are to be found in *Silex Scintillans*. It is rightly claimed by many critics that Vaughan's debt to Herbert is greater than that owed by any English poet to another.

PEACE

My soul, there is a country
Far beyond the stars,
Where stands a winged sentry
All skilful in the wars,
There above noise, and danger   5
Sweet peace sits crowned with smiles,
And one born in a manger
Commands the beauteous files,
He is thy gracious friend,
And (O my soul awake!)   10
Did in pure love descend
To die here for thy sake,
If thou canst get but thither,
There grows the flower of peace,
The rose that cannot wither,   15
Thy fortress, and thy ease;
Leave then thy foolish ranges;
For none can thee secure,
But one, who never changes,
Thy God, thy life, thy cure.   20

GLOSSARY

3 *winged sentry*: an archangel on guard

6 *crowned with smiles*: Peace is sitting on a throne wearing a crown of smiles

7–8 *one born … files*: the infant Christ commands splendid ranks of angels, who are there to preserve the peace of Heaven

17 *ranges*: wanderings

GUIDELINES

Here life is seen as a pilgrimage. Humans are never fully happy on earth. They are restless wanderers on their way to a happy country. This is the Heaven that awaits them at the end of their journey, which will take them 'Far beyond the stars'. Peace presents a vision of humankind's eternal, unchanging final home.

Almost all of Vaughan's most celebrated poems have the human being's relationship with God as their central theme. In his most famous poem, *The Retreate*, he sees life as a journey which takes him away from the happiness and innocence of early childhood, when he was close to God. He was even closer to God before his birth: coming into the world made him an exile from the heavenly home to which he can return only when he dies. In *Peace*, Vaughan gives us a vision of that home.

The speaker of the poem is addressing his own soul. He paints a delightful picture of Heaven, a country 'Far beyond the stars', whose inhabitants are permanently safe from trouble or danger of any kind. This is because Heaven is guarded by troops of armed angels. The essential quality of Heaven is lasting peace, which explains the title of the poem. The speaker tells his soul that only God can give it true peace and happiness.

At first reading, what is most surprising about the poem is the apparently contradictory nature of its images. Two strands of imagery may be identified. On the one hand, in Vaughan's paradise, we find peace enthroned as a monarch, crowned with smiles; peace is also a beautiful, undying flower. Again, this paradise is a place or state in which the restless, turbulent human soul will be for ever satisfied in the presence of God who presides over an unchanging eternity (lines 19–20).

On the other hand, it seems paradoxical that a poem entitled *Peace* should feature such striking military images as this one does. Heaven is guarded by a winged sentry with warlike skills. The infant of peace born in a manger commands the splendid angels drawn up in ranks like troops ('beauteous files'). Another military image is of heaven as a fortress (line 16).

How are we to understand the place of military images in a poem whose central theme is peace? To make sense of these images, we have to remember that Vaughan took his material from the Bible. His 'winged sentry' comes from the Book of Revelation. So, too, does the infant Christ who commands the ranks (the 'beauteous files') of angels. The Book of Revelation describes a conflict between Mary, the mother of Christ and Michael the Archangel on the one side, and Satan, in the form of a dragon, on the other. The following passage helps to explain Vaughan's military images in *Peace*:

So she brought forth a man child, which should rule all the nations with a rod
of iron, and her son was taken up unto God and to his throne ... and there was
a battle in heaven. Michael and his angels fought against the dragon ... And
the great dragon, that old serpent called the Devil and Satan, was cast out ...
and his angels were cast out with him.

It is clear that Vaughan's winged sentry is the Archangel Michael. He appears in
the poem as the defender of paradise against any possible invasion by Satan and
his followers. The military images are not in the poem to suggest violence or
aggression. Instead, they imply security and freedom from evil forces. The infant
who commands the angels and the winged archangel are there to preserve the
peace of Heaven, and to defend this peace against any renewal of the ancient
discord which once disturbed Heaven when Satan and his followers rebelled.

The poem, as one might expect, also has its images of peace. These images
are in the form of *conceits*. These are unusual and original comparisons.
The most striking one is the following:

> *There, above Noise, and danger*
> *Sweet peace sits crown'd with smiles* (lines 5–6).

Here we have an image of peace sitting on a throne wearing a crown of smiles. It
is a strange, surprising image. However, it captures our attention in a way that a
more straightforward image would not.

An important theme of the poem is expressed as a contrast. This is found in
the last eight lines:

> *If thou canst get but thither,*
> *There grows the flower of peace,*
> *The rose that cannot wither,*
> *Thy fortress, and thy ease;*
> *Leave then thy foolish ranges;*
> *For none can thee secure,*
> *But one, who never changes;*
> *Thy God, thy life, thy cure.*

Here we have one of Vaughan's favourite themes: the contrast between the
restless life of humans on earth and the security enjoyed by those in heaven, a
place free from change. The flower of heavenly peace and beauty cannot wither.

God is the one who never changes. By contrast, a person's soul on earth is constantly distracted by worries and small, unimportant things. This is why the poet tells his soul to abandon its wanderings and distractions ('foolish ranges').

Almost all Vaughan's poems have a moral. He believes that poetry should teach its readers a useful lesson. In Peace, the lesson is that humans can achieve happiness and make themselves secure by directing their lives towards God. Vaughan also tries to make his readers aware of the love and mercy of God for humankind.

> He is thy gracious friend
> And (O, my soul awake!)
> Did in pure love descend
> To die here for thy sake.

Notice the way in which Vaughan makes use of the sounds of words as well as the rhythm and movement of his lines to support his meanings. He conveys the peace and gentleness of paradise through a series of lines whose rhythms are quiet, almost caressing:

> Sweet peace sits crowned with smiles …
> There grows the flower of peace …

Notice the 's' sound. If you speak these lines, you will get a sense of quietness and relaxation. This is what the poet was trying to convey.

QUESTIONS

1 Some of the important images of the poem are not of peace, but of war. Can you explain this?

2 Consider the importance of contrast in the final eight lines of the poem.

3 What are the outstanding features of the Heaven Vaughan creates?

4 Comment on the significance of the title of the poem.

5 What is the moral of 'Peace'?

6 Discuss the way in which the sounds of the words, as well as the rhythm and movement, contribute to the meaning of the poem.

7 What are the main themes in the poem? How are these themes reflected?

8 The poet is clearly trying to teach a lesson. What is this lesson?

9 The poem is based on contrasts. Discuss some of these.

W.B. YEATS

1 8 6 5 – 1 9 3 9

BIOGRAPHY

William Butler Yeats was born in Sandymount, a Dublin suburb. His father was the artist John Butler Yeats, his mother a member of a well-to-do Sligo merchant family. When Yeats was nine the family moved to London, where he attended the Godolphin School, Hammersmith. In 1880, the family returned to Ireland and settled in Howth, where he attended the High School. He later studied at the College of Art in Dublin. Soon, however, his interest in art gave way to his enthusiasm for literature. From his late teens he was writing poetry with the active encouragement of his father. Early in his career, he began to explore mysticism and the occult, particularly Indian mysticism. This interest was to remain central to his outlook throughout his life. More significantly, however, he became active in helping to launch the movement known as the Irish Literary Renaissance. Encouraged by the veteran Fenian John O'Leary, he broadened his knowledge of Irish history and folklore. In the 1890s he was active in promoting the idea of a distinctively Irish literature for an Irish public.

During his visits to his uncle, George Pollexfen, in Sligo, he absorbed fairy lore and folk-tales. He read, in translation, Irish legends, the Cúchulainn saga and the stories of the Fianna, which inspired the poems in *The Rose* (1893), one of his early collections. The publication of *The Wanderings of Oisín and Other*

Poems in 1889 established him as a literary figure. The year before, he had met Maud Gonne, a committed Irish Nationalist, whose influence on his personal life and work was to be considerable, and who inspired his play *The Countess Kathleen* (1892) and a number of great poems. In 1896 he met Lady Gregory, the mistress of an estate at Coole in County Galway, where he composed many of his best poems, including the one which gives its name to his 1919 collection, *The Wild Swans at Coole*. In 1917, he bought an old Norman tower at Ballylee, close to Lady Gregory's house. He proposed marriage to Maud Gonne, whose husband, Major John MacBride, had been executed following the 1916 Rising. Having been turned down by her, he proposed to her daughter Iseult, again without success. In October 1917, his proposal of marriage was accepted by Georgie Hyde-Lees. He was 52 and she was 15.

Yeats's greatest poetry is to be found in *The Wild Swans at Coole* (1919); *Michael Robartes and the Dancer* (1921); *The Tower* (1928); *The Winding Stair and Other Poems* (1933) and *Last Poems* (1936–39). Following the establishment of the Irish Free State in 1922, Yeats took a lively interest in politics, becoming a member of the Irish Senate, and taking up such unpopular causes as divorce. In 1923 he was awarded the Nobel Prize for Literature. In the 1920s and 1930s he spent much time abroad, mainly for the sake of his health. In the 1930s, he took a sympathetic interest in Fascism, particularly in its Irish variety, the Blueshirt movement. His various autobiographical works are collected in *Autobiographies* (1955).

Yeats became seriously ill in France at the beginning of 1939 and died on 28 January of that year. He was buried in France, but his body was taken to Drumcliffe Churchyard near Sligo in 1948.

THE LAKE ISLE OF INNISFREE

I will arise and go now, and go to Innisfree,
And a small cabin build there, of clay and wattles made;
Nine bean-rows will I have there, a hive for the honey-bee,
And live alone in the bee-loud glade.

And I shall have some peace there, for peace comes dropping slow,   5
Dropping from the veils of the morning to where the cricket sings,
There midnight's all a glimmer, and noon a purple glow,
And evening full of the linnet's wings.

I will arise and go now, for always night and day
I hear lake water lapping with low sounds by the shore;   10
While I stand on the roadway, or on the pavements grey,
I hear it in the deep heart's core.

GLOSSARY

title *Innisfree*: an island in Lough Gill, County Sligo

1 *I will arise and go now*: Yeats seems to have had *Luke*, chapter 15, verse 18 in mind: 'I will arise and go to my father'. The prodigal son in the Gospel parable wants to return home, just as the the speaker in the poem does

2 *wattles*: flexible rods which can be interwoven and plastered with mud to form a building material

4 *glade*: open space in a wood

9 *always night and day*: an echo of *Mark*, chapter 5, verse 5: 'And always, night and day, he was in the mountains'

GUIDELINES

Yeats wrote the poem in London when he was twenty-five. As he walked through Fleet Street, a fountain in a shop window reminded him of the sound of lake water and thus revived his dream of living alone on the island in Lough Gill, finding wisdom and peace in the tradition of the ancient hermits.

It is easy to see why this became one of Yeats's most popular poems and why it has remained so. It is pleasant, fluent, not particularly demanding and rich in texture. It is remarkable for its beauty of sound and its relaxed rhythms. The movement, rhythm, repetition, alliteration and assonance combine to give the poem a soporific, dreamy quality, reminiscent of much Victorian escapist poetry in which ideal landscapes and states of living are evoked as alternatives to the unpleasantness of the real world.

The poem belongs to the early, romantic phase of Yeats's career, which was dominated by a quest for beauty in nature and in life. It celebrates a common and deep human impulse: the desire to find a way of escape from the sordid realities of city life into a pastoral utopia where, free from care, the fortunate recluse can enjoy the simple, peaceful life amid the beauties of a natural landscape. The attractions of the ideal island of Innisfree are heightened by the contrast with the drabness of London, with its 'pavements grey'.

QUESTIONS

1 Consider the poem as a pleasant piece of escapism. What does the speaker want to escape from?

2 The poem is remarkable for its beauty of sound and leisurely rhythms. How do such features help to convey the theme?

3 Do you think the kind of life imagined in the poem might prove satisfactory, and if so, in what ways? Would you enjoy the kind of life the speaker wants to create for himself?

4 This is perhaps the most popular of all Yeats's poems. Can you think of reasons for this?

5 Over time, Yeats came to dislike the poem. Can you suggest why?

6 In 'Sailing to Byzantium', Yeats imagines another ideal world. How do the two worlds compare? Which would you choose, and why?

THE WILD SWANS AT COOLE

The trees are in their autumn beauty,
The woodland paths are dry,
Under the October twilight the water
Mirrors a still sky;
Upon the brimming water among the stones   5
Are nine-and-fifty swans.

The nineteenth autumn has come upon me
Since I first made my count;
I saw, before I had well finished,
All suddenly mount   10
And scatter wheeling in great broken rings
Upon their clamorous wings.

I have looked upon those brilliant creatures,
And now my heart is sore.
All's changed since I, hearing at twilight,   15
The first time on this shore,
The bell-beat of their wings above my head,
Trod with a lighter tread.

Unwearied still, lover by lover,
They paddle in the cold   20
Companionable streams or climb the air;
Their hearts have not grown old;
Passion or conquest, wander where they will,
Attend upon them still.

But now they drift on the still water,   25
Mysterious, beautiful;
Among what rushes will they build,
By what lake's edge or pool
Delight men's eyes when I awake some day
To find they have flown away?   30

GLOSSARY

12 *clamorous*: noisy

18 *Trod ... tread*: walked with a lighter step.

GUIDELINES

This is the title-poem of a collection first published in 1917, when Yeats was fifty-two. At this point in his life, he was concerned with the exhausting effect of age on his imaginative powers. In the poem he reflects that he has been enjoying the beauty of the swans at Coole Park, the residence of his friend Lady Gregory, for nineteen years: his habit of counting them over that period reminds him of his own age. He is conscious of the gulf opening up between himself as the slave of time and the timeless nature represented by the swans ('their hearts have not grown old'). He ends the poem on a note of fear: one day, the swans, which embody his creative relationship with nature, will have gone elsewhere, leaving him desolate.

The poem is deeply symbolic. Like the subject of Keats's 'Ode to a Nightingale', Yeats's swans seem to defy time. They may age like Yeats, but they give the illusion of immortality. They are a Yeatsian symbol of eternity as they rise from the lake to wheel above him 'in great broken rings'. Unlike Yeats, and human beings in general, they can live, symbolically, on earth and in eternity: they are mortal ('lover by lover') and at the same time carry suggestions of immortality ('Unwearied still').

The meaning of the poem depends for a large extent on the relationship the speaker establishes between the swans and himself. The speaker, conscious of his advancing age, looks at the fifty-nine swans. He has been counting these swans for nineteen years. Over all that time they have, as if by a miracle, seemed to defy time ('Unwearied still ... Their hearts have not grown old'). The speaker knows that individual swans are no more immortal than he himself is, but they give the illusion of immortality: the pattern they establish survives.

Any interpretation of the poem must focus on the symbolism of the swans, without being over-precise about the meaning they generate. They anticipate the pattern of eternity as, before the speaker has finished counting them, they rise from the lake to wheel above him 'in great broken rings'. They link the 'still water' to the 'still sky', which is mirrored in it. Unlike people, they are able to live in two elements, air and water. More importantly, they are able to live (in the symbolic sense created by the poem) on earth as well as in eternity. They are mortal ('lover by lover') and yet give the impression of immorality ('Unwearied still').

Throughout the poem, we are conscious of the contrast between the speaker's sense of his own mortality and the perpetual youth and vitality enjoyed by the swans. In Stanza 2, for example, the swans resist the speaker's attempt to define them in terms of their number and to make them finite beings, when they assert their independence in a ritual flight symbolising their freedom from the constraints of time: 'All suddenly mount / And scatter wheeling in great broken rings'.

The emphasis of the third stanza is on the changeless character of the swans and the all too evident decline in the speaker's vitality which their animated movements underline for him:

> I have looked upon those brilliant creatures,
> And now my heart is sore.
> All's changed since I, hearing at twilight,
> The first time on this shore,
> The bell-beat of their wings above my head,
> Trod with a lighter tread.

The speaker's response to the contrast between his sense of mortality and the ageless vitality of the swans is a self-regarding sorrow: his heart is 'sore'. By the end of the poem, however, he has come to terms with his own ageing and the eternity symbolised by the swans, who are outside time.

The final stanza raises complex questions, suggested in the speaker's description of the swans as 'mysterious'. The contemplation of the mysterious creatures leads him to wonder where they will be, to delight men's eyes, when he awakes some day 'To find they have flown away'. In line 29, 'when I awake some day' cannot be taken literally. The speaker is not simply saying that some day he will awake to find that the swans have gone. The question then arises: what kind of awakening is he describing? Is he talking about awakening into death to find that the pattern of immortality represented by the swans has vanished, as he himself has become immortal? Or, given that the swans symbolise youthfulness, is he saying that their eventual flight from his life will signal his decline into old age and approaching death? Again the references to autumn and the passage of time ('The nineteenth autumn has come upon me') may suggest that the swans represent his youth and passionate past, or at least mirror this. The final stanza may, in the light of this, imply that when the speaker is old, perhaps dead (having awakened in eternity), the swans will delight other men in other places who enjoy the youth and passion that he has lost. The last two lines of Stanza 4 suggest that the passion or conquest associated with youth and vitality are an intimate part of their significance, that wherever they wander, these 'Attend upon them still'. Those human beings whose youth makes them capable of passion or conquest will always ('still') find in the swans a symbolic representation of their feelings and impulses.

The poem ends on the optimistic notion that the swans will always be symbols of beauty, love, youth and vitality. This reading is not universally accepted. Some interpreters see the poem as ending on a note of pessimism, and expressing the fear that the day will come when the swans, symbolising the speaker's creative relationship with nature, will desert him, leaving him bereft of inspiration and creativity.

QUESTIONS

1 The autumn setting is important. Why?
2 What does the counting of the swans signify?
3 What meaning do the swans have for the speaker?
4 The poem is partly based on a contrast between the speaker and the swans. What is this contrast? Mention some other contrasts in the poem.
5 Why is the speaker troubled as he contemplates the swans?
6 Does he have reason to envy them?
7 Do you think that the poem is more about the speaker than about the swans?
8 In what sense is this poem about time and eternity?
9 Consider some of the resemblances between this poem and 'Sailing to Byzantium'.
10 Is the ending of the poem hopeful or sad? Explain your answer.

AN IRISH AIRMAN FORESEES HIS DEATH

I know that I shall meet my fate
Somewhere among the clouds above;
Those that I fight I do not hate,
Those that I guard I do not love;
My country is Kiltartan Cross,   5
My countrymen Kiltartan's poor,
No likely end could bring them loss
Or leave them happier than before.
Nor law, nor duty bade me fight,
Nor public men, nor cheering crowds,   10
A lonely impulse of delight
Drove to this tumult in the clouds;
I balanced all, brought all to mind,
The years to come seemed waste of breath,
A waste of breath the years behind   15
In balance with this life, this death.

GLOSSARY

title *An Irish Airman*: the subject of this poem is Major Robert Gregory

1–2 *I know ... above*: Yeats makes Gregory 'know' what the future holds for him.
To understand this we have to bear in mind that Gregory was reputed to possess
psychic second sight which gave him a premonition of death. Yeats believed that
people could possess this faculty, and admired it

4 *Those that I guard*: the Allied peoples in the First World War

5–6 *My country ... poor*: the Gregorys lived on the Coole estate, Kiltartan, County
Galway. Kiltartan Cross is a few miles from Coole

7 *No likely end*: no likely result of the war

9 *Nor law, nor duty bade me fight*: I enlisted neither because I was legally compelled
to do so, nor out of a sense of patriotic duty

10 *public men*: politicians whose warlike oratory encouraged young men to fight

11 *A lonely impulse of delight*: his impulse to join in the fight is lonely because it comes from within himself. He will choose a hero's death in a war which is otherwise without meaning for him. There is a sense in which Yeats presents the war purely as an opportunity for Gregory to gratify his impulse and to resolve his personal problems

16 *this life, this death*: Yeats makes Gregory see life and death as equivalent to each other. He will find his life's meaning in the manner of his death

GUIDELINES

This poem is part of Yeats's 1919 volume, *The Wild Swans at Coole*. Its subject is Major Robert Gregory, the only son of Lady Gregory. Like his mother, Gregory had been extremely close to Yeats. He learned Irish at Coole, his mother's place, and became a stage-designer for Yeats's plays at the Abbey Theatre. He was a member of the Royal Flying Corps during the First World War. In January, 1918, he was shot down when returning to base in Northern Italy. The sixteen lines of this poem are not a conventional lament for a dear friend, but a presentation, or definition, of Gregory as the perfect man of Yeats's imagination. From Yeats's point of view, the quality that best defined the perfect man was balance, and this quality is central to his presentation of Gregory. From his lofty position in the clouds, Gregory is able to view the war with detachment and poise. He is not motivated to fight by partisan political emotions: he neither hates the Germans nor loves the English (lines 3–4). He balances the future prospects of his poor countrymen living on or near his estate at Kiltartan, County Galway, against the outcome of the war, concluding that they will neither lose nor gain whether the war is lost or won (lines 7–8). Gregory's detachment is further shown in his indifference to cheering crowds encouraging men such as himself to go to war and to the warlike speeches of politicians (line 10). Instead, he is able to resolve the tensions of his life by finding fulfilment in the 'tumult in the clouds', which will inevitably lead to his extinction. Yeats sees Gregory as a man fated to find his ultimate delight in the experience of death in life. Given his hero's impulse to balance 'all' at the expense of life itself, it is appropriate that Yeats should ask in another poem, *In Memory of Major Robert Gregory*, 'What made us dream that he could comb grey hair?'

The structural impulse behind the poem is indicated in line 13: 'I balanced all, brought all to mind'. Yeats makes his speaker take a balanced, unemotional view of his involvement in the war. This involvement is explained in four remarkable lines:

Nor law, nor duty bade me fight,
Nor public men, nor cheering crowds,
A lonely impulse of delight
Drove to this tumult in the clouds.

The lines are all the more remarkable when we consider the historical background against which they were written. Young men went to war because they were conscripted (by 'law') or because they saw it as their 'duty' to fight for their country. Alternatively, many of them were caught up in a patriotic surge, created by the passionate speeches of politicians ('public men') who had launched the war and were willing to sacrifice the youth of all nations to keep it going. This patriotic nationalism was further inflamed by the multitudes who cheered the doomed young men on to their deaths — the 'cheering crowds' of the poem. The speaker of Yeats's poem is unmoved by the emotions generated by the public rhetoric of war and the mass hysteria of patriotic crowds. These themes were rehearsed in innumerable war-poems of the period — many poets were prepared to debase their art in the service of propaganda by supplying recruiting verses to correspond to the government's recruiting posters. Most of the pro-war poetry is simple-minded in the extreme. The following from John Oxenham's *Helpful Verses for the Dark Days of War* is typical:

He died as few men get a chance to die—
Fighting to save a world's morality.
He died the noblest death a man can die,
Fighting for God, and Right, and Liberty—
And such a death is immortality.

To return to Yeats's poem, the speaker's participation in the war has nothing to do with such impulses, or with a belief in whatever goal the war was supposed to achieve, or with the notion that one side was right and the other wrong. He is above and beyond such absurd oppositions, having neither enthusiasm for the British cause nor contempt for the German one: 'Those that I fight I do not hate / Those that I guard I do not love'. His detachment is reinforced when he is able to view the conflict from the skies. His own point of view on the war is that of the poor country people living near the Gregory family estate in County Galway. For them, as for him, there will be neither loss nor happiness whatever the outcome of the war.

The war has, however, a purpose for the speaker. It gives him a splendid opportunity to resolve his own tensions, to live with the utmost intensity and to experience the paradox of death in life, which will give him his greatest fulfilment. His decision to fight, and die, in the skies is made coldly, rationally and without passion. His experience of death will not, however, be without passion: it will involve both delight and 'tumult'. Gregory thus becomes the kind of man Yeats most admired: one who can combine passion and detachment, joy and loneliness.

QUESTIONS

1 Describe the speaker's attitude to the war. Does he think it is worthwhile? Give your own responses to the ideas expressed by the speaker.
2 Consider the idea of balance as central to the poem.
3 Yeats greatly admired Major Robert Gregory, the subject of the poem. Does the poem suggest why?
4 Does the speaker emerge as a self-centred, even selfish man? Explain.
5 Does the poem give the impression of a man who feels superior to those around him?
6 How would you describe the tone of the poem?
7 Can this be described as an anti-war poem?
8 Given his attitude to the parties fighting the war, do you think the speaker was justified in becoming involved?

READING
UNSEEN POETRY

Reading a poem is an activity in which your mind, your beliefs and your feelings are called into play. As you read, you work to create the poem's meaning from the words and images offered to you by the poet. And the process takes a little time, so be patient. However, the fact that poems are generally short – much shorter than most stories, for example – allows you to read and reread a poem many times over.

Begin with the title. What expectations does it set up in you? What does it remind you of? As you read a poem, jot down your responses. These jottings may take the form of words or phrases from the poem which you feel are important, although you may not be able to say why this is so. Write questions, teasing out the literal meaning of a word or a phrase. Write notes or commentaries as you go, expressing your understanding. Record your feelings. Record your resistance to, or your approval of, any aspect of the poem – its statements, the choice of words, the imagery, the tone, the values it expresses.

Jot down any association brought to mind by any element of the poem, such as a word. Note any ideas suggested by any part of a poem – a word, a phrase, an image, the rhythm or tone, or the title. Be alert to combinations of words and patterns of repetition. Look for those words or images that carry emotional or symbolic force. Try to understand their effect. Note down other poems which the unseen poem reminds you of. In this way, you create a territory in which the poem can be read and understood.

Don't feel that you have to supply all the answers asked of you by a poem. In a class situation, confer with your fellow students. Words and images will resonate in different ways for different people. Readers bring their own style, ideas and experiences to every encounter with a poem. Sharing ideas and adopting a collaborative approach to the reading of a new poem will open out the poem's possibilities beyond what you, or any individual, will achieve alone.

Poems frequently work by way of hints, suggestions or associations. The unstated may be as important as the stated. Learn to live with ambiguity. Learn to enjoy the uncertainty of poetry. Don't be impatient if a poem doesn't 'make sense' to you. Most readers interpret and work on poems with more success than they know or admit! Learning to recognise your own competence and trusting in it is an important part of reading poems in a fruitful way. Remember that reading is an active process and that your readings are provisional and open to reconsideration.

In an examination, you will not be able to talk with your fellow students or return to the poem many times, over a couple of days. Trust yourself. In an examination the poem may be new to you, but the reading of poems is not. Draw on your experience of creating meaning. Poetry works to reveal the world in new ways. D. H. Lawrence said: 'The essential quality of poetry is that it makes a new effort of attention and "discovers" a new world within the known world'. In an examination, you are looking to show how a poem, and your reading of it, presents a new view of the world. Read the poem over, noting and jotting as you do so, and then focus on different aspects of the poem. The questions set on the poem will help direct your attention.

Here are some suggested ways into a poem. They are not exhaustive or definitive.

THE WORDS OF THE POEM

Remember that every word chosen by a poet suggests that another word was rejected.

In poetry some words are so charged with meaning that literal or everyday meaning gives way to their figurative or poetic meaning. Often there are one or two words in a poem that carry a weight of meaning: these words can be read in a variety of ways that open up the poem for you.

Here are some questions you can ask:
  1 Are the words in the poem simple or complex, concrete or abstract?
  2 How are they clustered into phrases?
  3 Are there any obvious patterns of word usage, for example words that refer to colours, or verbs that suggest energy and force?
  4 Is there a pattern in the descriptive words used by the poet?
  5 Are there key words – words that carry a symbolic or emotional force – or a clear set of associations? (Does the poet play with these associations by calling them into question or subverting them?)
  6 Do patterns of words establish any contrasts or oppositions, for example night and day, winter and summer, joy and sorrow, love and death?

THE MUSIC AND MOVEMENT OF THE POEM

In relation to the sounds and rhythms of the poem, note such characteristics as the length of the lines or the presence or absence of rhyme. Consider how sound patterns add to the poem's texture and meaning. For example, do the sound patterns create a sense of hushed stillness or an effect of forceful energy?

Ask yourself some or all of the following questions:
  1 What is the pattern of line length in the poem?
  2 What is the pattern of rhyme?
  3 Is there a pattern to vowel sounds and length? What influence might this have on the rhythm of the poem or the feelings conveyed by it?
  4 Are there patterns of consonant sounds, including alliteration? What is their effect?
  5 Are there changes in the poem's rhythm? Where and why do these occur?

THE VOICE OF THE POEM

Each poem has its own voice. When you read a poet's work, you can often recognise a distinctive poetic voice. This may be in the poem's rhythms or in the viewpoint it expresses. Sometimes it is most evident in the tone of voice of the poem. Sometimes you are taken by the warmth of a poetic voice, or its coldness and detachment, or its tone of amused surprise. Try to catch the distinctive characteristic of the voice of the poem as you read. Decide if it is a man's voice or a woman's voice and what this might mean. Try to place the voice in a context. This may help you to understand the assumptions in the poem's statements, or the emotional force of those statements.

THE IMAGERY OF THE POEM

Images are the descriptive words and phrases used by poets to speak to our senses. They are mostly visual in quality (word pictures) but they can also appeal to our senses of touch, smell and hearing. Images and patterns of imagery are key elements in the way that poems convey meanings. They create moods, capture emotions and suggest or call out feelings in the readers.

Ask yourself these questions:

1 Are there patterns of images in the poem?
2 What kind of world is suggested by the images of the poem – familiar or strange, fertile or barren, secure or threatening, private or public, calm or stormy, generous or mean? (Images often suggest contrasts or opposites.)
3 What emotions are associated with the images of the poem?
4 What emotions, do you think, inspired the choice of images?
5 What emotions do the images cause in you?
6 If there are images which are particularly powerful, why do they carry the force they do?
7 Do any of the images have the force of a symbol?
8 What is the usual meaning of the symbol?
9 What is its meaning in the poem?

THE STRUCTURE OF THE POEM

There are endless possibilities for structuring a poem. The obvious structures of a poem are the lines and the stanzas. Short lines give a sense of tautness to a poem. Long lines can create a conversational feel and allow for shifts and changes in rhythm. Rhyme and the pattern of rhyme influence the structure of a poem.

The poem is also structured by the movement of thought. This may or may not coincide with line and stanza divisions. Words like 'while', 'then' and 'and' help you trace the line of thought or argument as it develops through the poem.

In narrative poems, a simple form of structure is provided by the story itself and the sequence of events it describes. Another simple structure is one in which the poet describes a scene and then records his/her response to it. Or a poem may be built on a comparison or a contrast. The structure may also come from a series of parallel statements or a series of linked reflections.

However, the structure of a poem can be quite subtle, dependent on such things as word association or changes in emotions. Be alert to a change of focus or a shift of thought or emotion in the poem. Quite often there is a creative tension between the stanza structure – the visual form of the poem – and the emotional or imaginative structure of the poem. For this reason, be alert to turning points in poems. These might be marked by a pause, by a change in imagery or by a variation in rhythm

EXAM ADVICE FROM THE DEPARTMENT OF EDUCATION AND SCIENCE

The Department of Education and Science published this advice to students on answering the unseen poem in the Leaving Certificate Examination:

> *As the unseen poem on the paper will more than likely be unfamiliar to you, you should read it a number of times (at least twice) before attempting your answer. You should pay careful attention to the introductory note printed above the text of the poem.*

Other advice from the Department of Education includes the following explanation of terms and questions, which are relevant to the answering of the questions on the unseen poem:

Do you agree with this statement?

You are free to agree in full or in part with the statement offered. But you must deal with the statement in question – you cannot simply dismiss the statement and write about a different topic of your choice.

Write a response to this statement (or Discuss)

As above, your answer can show the degree to which you agree or disagree with a statement or point of view. You can also deal with the impact the text made on you as a reader.

What does the poem say to you about …?

What is being asked for here is **your** understanding/reading of the poem. It is important that you show how your understanding comes from the text of the poem, its language and imagery.

LAST WORD

The really essential part in reading a poem is that you try to meet the poet halfway. Bring your intelligence and your emotions to the encounter with a poem and match the openness of the poet with an equal openness of mind and heart. And when you write about a poem, give your honest assessment.

GUIDELINES FOR ANSWERING QUESTIONS ON POETRY

Many of the questions asked in the poetry section of Leaving Cert English ask for your personal response to the work of a particular poet. Questions may be phrased in many different ways, such as: 'Do you like the poetry of ...' , 'Poet X: a personal response', 'What impact did the poetry of Poet Y have on you as a reader?'. However, they are all essentially looking for the same thing – evidence that you have engaged fully with the work of the poet under discussion.

It is important to remember that each reader of a poem responds in an individual way. It may be, too, that the work of a particular poet moves us in ways that we can never hope to understand fully. But having said that, if your answer is to become more than just a series of vague impressions about the poems, there are aspects of a poet's work that you should consider when forming a response. The following suggestions may help but they are not intended to be exhaustive or prescriptive.

THEMES

A poet may make an impact on you as a reader because of the **themes** he or she chooses to write about. Often we respond to what we read, initially at least, because we find a reflection there of our own views and concerns. Since relationships are important in our lives, you may respond deeply to the exploration of human relationships in the poems of Sylvia Plath and Michael Longley.

Your response may be influenced by how your own understanding of great human themes, such as love or death, has been enriched by reading the work of a certain poet, for example John Donne or Thomas Hardy.

You may find the descriptions of the natural world in the poems of Elizabeth Bishop or Gerard Manley Hopkins exhilarating and attractive. You may respond positively to the way in which these descriptions lead them to a deeper understanding of themselves or of God.

You might also respond, of course, to a poet's themes because they are unfamiliar or even unusual. A good poet will enable the reader to imagine what it is like to be in a certain situation or to experience the world as he or she does, even if that world seems strange at times. So you may find Hopkins' depiction of mental torment, or T. S. Eliot's depiction of sordid city landscapes, or the historical situations recreated in the poems of W. B. Yeats interesting for these or other reasons.

Remember that your response should show that you have considered the poet's choice of theme carefully. It is not enough to present a list of the issues dealt with in the poems. In your preparation for the exam you should consider how each poet develops the themes chosen, what questions are raised in your mind as you read and whether the issues are resolved or not. Bear in mind that themes are sometimes complex (in fact sometimes it is their very complexity that we respond to) and are open to more than one interpretation.

THE POET'S PERSONALITY OR OUTLOOK

Since poems are often written out of a poet's inner urgency, they can reveal a great deal about the personality of the poet. You may find that you respond to what poets reveal about themselves in their work almost as much as you would to an autobiography. Elizabeth Bishop's poems about her childhood convey a sensitive, observant person whose experiences will affect her for the rest of her life. Sylvia Plath reveals her emotional anguish in painfully honest terms.

Read the work of each of the poets carefully with this in mind. Can you build up a profile of each poet from what he or she has written, from his or her own personal voice?

It may also be that you like the work of a poet for the contrasting reason that he or she goes beyond personal revelation to create other voices, other lives. You may find the voices that speak in T. S. Eliot's poems make an impact on you for this reason. Many of Michael Longley's and Thomas Hardy's poems too recreate the experience of former times.

THE POET'S USE OF LANGUAGE

Your response to the work of any poet will almost certainly be influenced by how he or she uses language.

In preparing for the examination you should examine carefully the individual **images** or **patterns of imagery** used by each of the eight poets on your course. When you write about imagery, try to analyse how the particular poet you are dealing with creates the effects he or she does. Does he or she appeal to our senses – our visual, tactile and aural senses, and our senses of taste and smell? How did you respond? Do you find the images effective in conveying theme or emotion?

Do the images appeal to you because their clarity and vividness allow you to visualise the scene (in a poem by Wordsworth, say), or because they leave you baffled and puzzled in an exciting way, like some of the images of Emily Dickinson or Michael Longley, for instance?

Are the images created by the use of simile and metaphor? Can you say why these particular comparisons were chosen by the poet? Do you find them precise, surprising, fresh?

If the poet makes use of symbol or personification, consider how these devices might add to a poem's richness so that it acquires a universal significance.

You may find you like the way a poet blends poetic and conversational language, or how he or she uses language both to denote (to signify) and to connote (to suggest).

You may respond positively to a poet's simplicity of expression as in Thomas Hardy's poems, or to a sense that a poet's use of complex language reflects complex ideas, as in the poems of John Donne.

THE SOUNDS OF POETRY

Many people find that it is the sound of poetry that they respond to most. It is an ancient human characteristic to respond to word patterns like rhyme or musical effects such as rhythm so sound may be one of the aspects of a particular poet's work that appeals to you most.

Poets use sound effects such as alliteration, assonance and onomatopoeia for many reasons – some thematic, some for emotive effect, some merely because of the sheer pleasure of creating pleasant musical word patterns. Look carefully at how each of the eight poets makes use of sound and try to suggest why they are doing so. Your response will be much richer if based on close reading and attention to the poems.

POETRY AND THE EMOTIONS

We may respond intellectually to the themes of a poem, but very often it is the emotional intensity of a poem that enables us to engage with it most fully. At their best poems celebrate what it is to be human, with all that being human suggests, including confronting our deepest fears and anxieties.

The tone of a poem conveys the emotions that lie behind it. All of the elements in a poem may be used to convey tone and emotion. A poet's choice of imagery and the language he or she uses can be very expressive. For example, Yeats' imagery can express the contempt he feels for certain aspects of society around him, while T. S. Eliot's choice of imagery suggests the alienation he senses in modern life.

Remember, too, that the use of sound conveys emotions well. Look at the work of the different poets with this in mind.

What corresponding emotions does the work of each poet on your course create in you as a reader? Do you feel consoled, uplifted, disturbed, perhaps even alienated? Does the poet succeed in conveying his or her feelings, if indeed that is what is intended in the poem? These are questions you should consider in preparing to form your response.

CONCLUSION

It is worth remembering that you will be rewarded for your attempts to come to terms with the work of the poets you have studied in a personal and responsive way. This may entail a heartfelt negative response, too. But even a negative response must display close reading and should pay attention to specific aspects of the poems. Do not feel that you have to conform to the opinions of others – including the opinions expressed in this book!

Read the question carefully. Some questions may direct your attention to specific elements of a poet's work. Make sure you deal with these in your answer.

Some questions may simply invite you to include some aspects of a poet's work in your response. It would be unwise to ignore any hints as to how to proceed!

You will be required to support your answer by reference to or quotation from the poems chosen. Remember that long quotations are hardly ever necessary.

The Department of Education and Science has published the following advice to students on answering the question on poetry: *It is a matter of judgement as to which of the poems will best suit the question under discussion and candidates should not feel a necessity to refer to all of the poems they have studied.*

As in all of the questions in the examination, you will be marked using the following criteria:

1 *Clarity of purpose (30% of marks available)* This is explained by the Department of Education and Science as 'engagement with the set task' – in other words, are you answering the question you have been asked? Is your answer relevant and focused?

2 *Coherence of delivery (30% of marks available)* Here you are assessed on your 'ability to sustain the response over the entire answer'. Is there coherence and continuity in the points you are making? Are the references you choose to illustrate your points appropriate?

3 *Efficiency of language use (30% of marks available)* The Department of Education and Science explains this as the 'management and control of language to achieve clear communication'. Aspects of your writing such as vocabulary, use of phrasing, and fluency – your writing style – will be taken into account.

4 *Accuracy of mechanics (10% of marks available)* Your levels of accuracy in spelling and grammar are what count here. Always leave some time during the exam to read over your work – you are bound to spot at least some errors.

Good luck!

GLOSSARY OF TERMS

ALLITERATION

This is a figure of speech in which consonants, especially at the beginning of words, are repeated. The term itself means 'repeating and playing upon the same letter'. Alliteration is a common feature of poetry in every period of literary history. Here is an example from 'Felix Randal' by Gerard Manley Hopkins: 'Who have watched his mould of man, big-boned and hardy-handsome'.

ALLUSION

An allusion is a reference to a person, place or event or to another work of art or literature. The purpose of allusion is to get the reader to share an experience which has significant meaning for the writer. When a writer makes use of allusion, he or she takes it for granted that the reader will possess the background knowledge necessary to understand its significance in the context of the work. In many cases, the significance of the allusion becomes clearer as the poem evolves. By the end of 'The Tollund Man' by Seamus Heaney, for instance, readers will have understood the poet's purpose in the first two lines 'Some day I will go to Aarhus / To see his peat-brown head'.

AMBIGUITY

Ambiguous words, phrases or sentences are capable of being understood in two or more possible senses. In many poems, ambiguity is part of the poet's method and is essential to the meaning of the poem. A poem like Hopkins' 'The Windhover' yields up a rich store of multiple meanings. The 'dapple-dawn-drawn Falcon' may be drawn (etched, outlined) against the dappled dawn, or drawn upwards into the dawn.

ASSONANCE

This is the repetition of identical or similar vowel sounds, especially in stressed syllables, in a sequence of nearby words. Assonance can contribute significantly to the meaning of a poem. A good example is John Keats's use of the recurring long 'i' in the opening lines of 'Ode on a Grecian Urn': 'Thou still unravish'd bride of quietness / Thou foster-child of silence and slow time'.

BALLAD

Ballads were originally songs, transmitted orally. They commented on life by telling stories in a popular style. In ballads, the attention of the readers is concentrated on the story and the characters. Every ballad must have a meaning that can easily be grasped by the reader. 'Sir Patrick Spens' is one of the most celebrated of all ballads. Its first two stanzas exemplify the main features found in almost all ballads: the abrupt and arresting opening, the economical sketch of the setting and action and the sharp transition from narrative to dialogue and back again. Other features of ballads are refrains, repetitions and simplicity of diction.

COLLOQUIALISM

A colloquial word or phrase is one that is used in everyday speech and writing. The colloquial style is plain and relaxed. At the end of the eighteenth century, Wordsworth declared that his aim was to imitate, as far as possible, what he called 'the very language of men'. In much poetry of the twentieth and twenty-first centuries, there is an acceptance of colloquialism, even slang, as a medium of poetic expression. The poems of Philip Larkin frequently exemplify this idea.

CONCEIT

The term 'conceit' is generally used for figures of speech that establish arresting parallels between objects or situations which, at first glance, seem to have little or nothing in common. All comparisons discover a likeness in things unalike. A comparison becomes a conceit when the poet forces us to concede likeness, while at the same time we are strongly conscious of unlikeness. The conceit is a characteristic device of the seventeenth-century metaphysical poets, among them Donne and Herbert. A famous modern conceit is found in T. S. Eliot's 'Prufrock': 'Let us go then you and I / When the evening is spread out against the sky / Like a patient etherised upon a table'.

CONVENTION

This is the name given to any aspect of a literary work which author and readers accept as normal and to be expected in that kind of writing. For example, it is a convention that a sonnet has fourteen lines that rhyme in a certain pattern. By convention, the ballad has a particular kind of diction. Sometimes conventions are abandoned or replaced. Eighteenth-century poetic diction, for example, gave way to a more 'natural' form of expression.

DICTION

Diction is the vocabulary used by a writer – his or her selection of words. Until the beginning of the nineteenth century, poets wrote in accordance with the principle that the diction of poetry had to differ, often significantly, from that of current speech. There was, in other words, a certain sort of 'poetic' diction which, by avoiding commonplace words and expressions, was supposed to lend dignity to the poem and its subject. This is entirely contrary to modern practice.

GENRE

The term is used to signify a particular literary species or form. Traditionally, the important genres were epic, tragedy, comedy, elegy, satire, lyric and pastoral. Until modern times, critics tended to distinguish carefully between the various genres and writers were expected to follow the rules prescribed for each. For example, if a poet wrote an epic, it was assumed that his or her language would be dignified, in keeping with the heroic nature of the subject, and that he or she would use epic similes, often many lines in length. Epics were also expected to feature long descriptive passages.

IMAGERY

This is a term with a very wide application. When we speak of the imagery of a poem, we refer to all its images taken collectively. The poet C. Day Lewis puts the matter well when he describes an image as 'a picture made out of words'. If we consider imagery in its narrow and popular sense, it signifies descriptions of visible objects and scenes, as, for example, in Wordsworth's account of the landscape in 'Tintern Abbey' (such as the pastoral farms, and the wreaths of smoke sent up in silence from among the trees). In its wider sense, imagery signifies figurative language, especially metaphor and simile.

LYRIC

Originally a lyric was a song performed to the accompaniment of a lyre. The term is now used to signify any relatively short poem in which a single speaker, not necessarily representing the poet, expresses feelings and thoughts in a personal and subjective fashion. Most poems are either lyrics or feature large lyrical elements.

METAPHOR AND SIMILE

These are the two commonest figures of speech in poetry. A simile contains two parts – a subject that is the focus of attention, and another element that is introduced for the sake of emphasising some quality in the subject. In a simile, the poet uses some such word as 'like' or 'as' to show that a comparison is being made. Wordsworth's sonnet 'It is a beauteous evening' begins with a particularly effective simile ('It is a beauteous evening, calm and free, / The holy time is quiet as a nun / Breathless with adoration'). Here the evening is being compared to a praying nun. A number of resemblances justify the comparison: both the nun and the evening are calm, and the dark habit of the nun suggests the enveloping darkness of evening. A deeper purpose of the simile is to connect the devotion of the nun with the 'beauteous evening', thus conveying a sense of the sacred mystery the poet feels as he contemplates the evening.

Metaphor differs from simile only in omitting the comparative word ('like' or 'as'). If in a simile someone's teeth are like pearls, in a metaphor they *are* pearls. While in the case of a simile the comparison is openly proclaimed as such, in the case of a metaphor the comparison is implied. A metaphor is capable of a greater range of suggestiveness than a simile and its implications are wider and richer. The simile, by its very nature (with the 'like' or 'as' formula), is limited to a compara- tively small area of suggestion. One advantage of metaphor is its tendency to establish numerous relationships between the two things being compared. T. S. Eliot's 'Gerontion' provides a good example. An old man says he is 'A dull head among windy spaces'. The reader is left to discover why the old man sees himself as a cliff or point of land, and elements of resemblance soon suggest themselves. The fact that the old man is like a cliff suggests that he is lonely, assailed by troubles as a cliff is by winds, but at the same time unthinking and unresponsive.

ONOMATOPOEIA

This involves the use of words that resemble, or enact, the very sounds they imitate. If a poet tries to make the sound reflect the meaning, he or she is using onomatopoeia. In 'Inversnaid' Hopkins uses onomatopoeic words to mimic his meaning ('Degged with dew, dappled with dew / Are the groins of the braes that the brook treads through'). In many cases, as in this example from Hopkins, the onomatopoeic effect is achieved through the use of alliteration.

PARADOX

This is an apparently self-contradictory statement which, on further consid- eration, is found to contain an essential truth. Paradox is so intrinsic to human nature that poetry rich in paradox is valued as a reflection of the central truths of human experience. A prime example of paradox is Wordsworth's consistent attempt to show that the common was really uncommon, an example followed by Kavanagh in 'Advent' ('And the newness that was in every stale thing / When we looked at it as children'). Paradox is at the centre of the Christian faith, a truth memorably conveyed by T. S. Eliot in 'East Coker' as he meditates on the relationship between God and the soul ('Our only health is the disease / If we obey the dying nurse').

SIMILE

See 'metaphor and simile'.

SONNET

This is a single-stanza lyric, consisting of fourteen lines. These fourteen lines are just long enough to make possible the fairly complex development of a single theme, and short enough to test the poet's gift for concentrated expression. The poet's freedom is further restricted by a demanding rhyme scheme and a conventional metrical form (five strong stresses in each line). The greatest sonnets are those in which the poet has overcome the limitations of the form and achieved the great aim of reconciling freedom of expression, variety of rhythm, mood and tone and richness of imagery with adherence to a rigid set of conventions.

English poets have traditionally written one of two kinds of sonnet – the Petrarchan and the Shakespearean. The Petrarchan sonnet, favoured by Milton and Wordsworth, falls into two divisions – the octave (eight lines rhyming abba, abba) and the sestet (six lines generally rhyming cde, cde). The octave generally presents a problem, situation or incident; the sestet resolves the problem or comments on the situation or incident. In contrast, the Shakespearean sonnet consists of three quatrains (groups of four lines rhyming abab, cdcd, efef) and a rhyming couplet (gg).

STYLE

This may be defined as the manner of expression characteristic of a writer – that is, his or her particular way of saying things. Consideration of style involves an examination of the writer's diction, figures of speech, order of words, tone and feeling, rhythm and movement. Traditionally, styles were classified according to three categories: high (formal or learned), middle and low (plain). Convention required that the level of style be appropriate to the speaker, the subject matter, the occasion which inspired the poem and the literary genre. A modern critic, Northrop Frye, suggests that styles could be classified under two broad headings: (a) demotic style, modelled on the language, rhythms and associations of everyday speech, and (b) hieratic style, involving formal, elaborate expression, with the aim of separating literary language from ordinary speech.

SYMBOL

A symbol is anything that stands for something else. In this sense, all words are symbols because they signify things other than themselves. Literary symbolism, however, comes about when the *objects* signified by the words stand in turn for things other than themselves. At a simple level, symbolism is familiar to almost everybody because certain conventional symbols are universally popular. Objects commonly associated with fixed ideas or qualities have come to symbolise these: for example, the cross is the primary Christian symbol, and the dove is a symbol of peace. Colour symbols have no fixed meaning, but derive their significance from a context: green may signify innocence or Irish patriotism or envy. The literary symbol is not a token with a precise meaning to be pinned down and accurately described. Some poets use symbols as essentially private tokens so that even the context can do little to help them to generate their meanings. When Yeats, for example, does this, he sets his readers some difficult problems of interpretation.

TONE

When one is trying to describe the tone of a poem, it is best to think of every poem as a spoken, rather than a written, exercise. A poem has at least one speaker who is addressing somebody or something. In some poems, the speaker can be thought of as meditating aloud, talking to himself or herself. We, the readers, catch him or her in the act and overhear them. Every speaker must inevitably have an attitude to the person or object being addressed or talked about, and must also see himself or herself in some relationship with that person or object. This attitude or relationship will determine the tone of the utterance. Tone may thus be defined as the expression of a literary speaker's attitude to, and relationship with, the listener or the subject. In real life, a person's attitude to another is often revealed in the tone of voice of that person and in the words chosen. A sensitive reading aloud of most poems will soon reveal the tone of a speaker's utterance. The opening lines of Yeats's 'September 1913' are ironical and contemptuous in tone. In 'Tintern Abbey' the speaker addresses his sister in tones of love and admiration and talks of nature in solemn, prayerful, reverent tones, in phrases borrowed from works of Christian piety.